Jacob Mendes De Solla

A Vocabulary of the Pentateuch

Containing all the Words of the Five Books in their Primitive Forms

Jacob Mendes De Solla

A Vocabulary of the Pentateuch
Containing all the Words of the Five Books in their Primitive Forms

ISBN/EAN: 9783337188580

Printed in Europe, USA, Canada, Australia, Japan

Cover: Foto ©Andreas Hilbeck / pixelio.de

More available books at **www.hansebooks.com**

כל דברי התורה

A

VOCABULARY

OF

THE PENTATEUCH;

CONTAINING

ALL THE WORDS OF THE FIVE BOOKS IN THEIR PRIMITIVE FORMS,
WITH AN ENGLISH TRANSLATION;

FOLLOWED BY

AN ALPHABETICAL INDEX OF THE HEBREW WORDS,

WITH REFERENCES TO THE PAGE WHERE EACH MAY BE FOUND IN
THE VOCABULARY.

DESIGNED AS A CLASS-BOOK,

AND AT THE SAME TIME TO ANSWER THE PURPOSE OF A SCHOOL DICTIONARY.

TO WHICH IS PREFIXED

A SYNOPSIS OF HEBREW GRAMMAR,

TO FACILITATE THE STUDY FOR BEGINNERS.

COMPILED BY
J. M. DE SOLLA.

PHILADELPHIA:
PRINTED FOR THE AUTHOR,
BY COLLINS, 705 JAYNE STREET.
1865.

"It is the fate of those who toil at the lower employments of life, to be rather driven by the fear of evil than attracted by the prospect of good; to be exposed to censure without hope or praise; to be disgraced by miscarriage, or punished for neglect, where success would have been without applause, and diligence without reward.

"Among these unhappy mortals is the writer of dictionaries, whom mankind have considered, not as the pupil, but the slave of science, the pioneer of literature, doomed only to remove rubbish and clear obstructions from the paths, through which Learning and Genius press forward to conquest and glory, without bestowing a smile on the humble drudge that facilitates their progress. Every other author may aspire to praise; the lexicographer can only hope to escape reproach; and even this negative recompense has been yet granted to very few."—DR. JOHNSON.

PREFACE.

The knowledge and study of the Hebrew language, in this age of general progress, has, like other sciences, also been more progressive.

Whether we receive the Holy Scriptures as the oracles of God, as all true believers do, or whether they are looked upon simply as records of past events, their value, and the advantage of being able to read them in the original tongue seem from day to day to be more recognized, not only by the Jewish nation, who have ever been the repository of that inestimable treasure, but even by the Christian scholar, who finds the study of Hebrew necessary, in order to penetrate into that fundamental structure upon which his faith is rested.

Israelites, also, who regarded the knowledge of the sacred tongue with comparative indifference, become more alive to its importance, and more dissatisfied with that superficial knowledge of the language which enables them merely to *read* their prayers as "an acquired precept of men." The truth becomes more and more apparent that the Hebrew language, if worth being studied at all, is worth being studied well and thoroughly; and the fact more palpable that the sacred volume is in the highest degree interesting and valuable, inasmuch as — exclusive of its religious and moral influence — it transmits to us the chronicles of the most remote antiquity; supplies the world with an infallible source of universal history and chronology; and possesses many attractions in the diver-

sified beauties of composition which **adorn its pages,** and
which have been celebrated by innumerable **writers** in all
ages and countries.

Every effort to promote the knowledge of **so valuable** a
work, and facilitate the study of the **language in** which it
was originally written can therefore not be **but commend-**
able; and the compiler of the present **volume trusts** that,
notwithstanding the numerous works on **Hebrew** Grammar now extant, this result of his labors **may** not be a
superfluous addition, but tend materially to **assist** the student in the acquisition of this important **branch of learning.**

In placing this Vocabulary before the **public, the** compiler makes no pretensions to novelty; yet **he believes** that
it will supply a real want to those who **impart, as** well as
to those who receive, instruction in the **Hebrew language.**
His long experience in the tuition of it, **has convinced** him
of the propriety of a practical knowledge of **the language**
preceding the theoretical study of it; **and it is the** acquisition of that practical knowledge which **this** vocabulary is chiefly intended to facilitate. In **the instruction**
of Hebrew, as well as in that of other **foreign languages,**
it has been the method of many teachers — **much** to the
detriment of their pupils — to plunge with **them at** once
into the tedious rules of grammar, **without having** furnished them previously with any practical **knowledge** of
the language they are to study. This, we **apprehend,** is
beginning at the wrong end. That the **student** should, at
the **beginning,** be furnished with the crude **materials** con-
stituting the structure of any language; that **his** memory
should be stocked with a considerable **number** of uncon-

nected words of which the language is composed, before any attempt is made to study the laws which regulate the use of that complicated composition, seems as natural as that a child learns to speak his mother-tongue long before he begins to learn its grammar. Let us suppose a student to be quite perfect in the rules of Hebrew grammar, and to be able to go through a series of conjugations and declensions, yet if he open his Bible and try to translate a portion of it, he will find himself at a loss, and scarcely be able to render one verse correctly, unless he is familiar with the primitive words and their import; while, on the other hand, if he has become master of the primary constituents of the text, a very superficial knowledge of the rules of grammar will enable him to understand almost any passage with comparative readiness and ease.

Under this conviction we have imposed upon ourselves the arduous and tedious task of the present compilation, trusting that it will lighten the labor of those who, like ourselves, are engaged in the tuition of the holy tongue, and promote the knowledge of it among those whose instruction is entrusted to our care.

As to the plan and arrangement of the work, we deem it necessary to say but little. The words, it will be perceived, are divided into three principal sections, of Nouns, Verbs, and Particles, the three primary or essential parts of speech, except the pronouns and numerals, which, being but few and of frequent occurrence, are given under separate heads, that they may be committed to memory before any other part. It will be further observed, that the words are arranged in the same order as they occur in

1*

the Scriptures, in order that the book may be used as a
manual in the translation of the Pentateuch.

The renderings do not in all cases represent the full
import of the **o**riginal, which could be·looked for only in
a more comprehensive dictionary. Our aim has been
chiefly to give the sense of the words as they are used in
the text from which they are quoted. Wherever they
admit of a different signification, it has been added; and
when such signification is of uncommon use, a figure has
been attached, with reference to the place, or one of the
places, where it is to be so rendered, confining our trans-
lations always to the limits of the *five books*, this being
only a *Vocabulary of the Pentateuch.*

Verbs, assuming different meanings in different conjugations, have been repeated as often as their meaning
varies — even those which retain the original force of the
root throughout, but have a different shade of meaning;
such as, רָאָה (1st form) *to see*, הֵרָאָה (2d form) *to appear*,
הַרְאָה (5th form) *to show*.

Verbs in the נִפְעַל have been given, sometimes in the
form of the infinitive absolute הִפָּעֵל, and sometimes with
the prefix נ as a sign of the second conjugation. The
form in which they occur in the text under consideration
has generally determined the choice.

Whenever a verb appears, either with omission of any
of its radicals, or with some servile letters added to it, the
whole radix has been placed by the side of it, so that in
all cases the learner may refer to some more explanatory
dictionary to gain such information as our limited space
did not allow us to impart.

An ALPHABETICAL INDEX, in which all the words of the

Vocabulary are repeated, has been added, with numbers attached, referring to the page in the Vocabulary where each word may be found, thus supplying, in some measure, the want of a Hebrew dictionary.

Lastly, a SYNOPSIS OF HEBREW GRAMMAR has been placed at the beginning, setting forth the principal rules necessary for beginners, which we believe will greatly increase the value of this little volume. It is of course not intended to represent a complete Hebrew grammar, but merely to furnish the student with the essential parts of it, and prepare him for the use of a more extensive work on that subject. After having gone through these fundamental rules, the learner, in his subsequent studies, will find himself like one erecting a building on a firm foundation, while he who takes hold of a complete grammar, and attempts to go through it regularly, will experience the difficulty of one who has to work on the foundation and superstructure at the same time.

With these prefatory observations in regard to the character of the work, it is offered to the public to make such use of it as their own discretion may suggest. If we may presume, however, to offer our fellow-laborers some advice founded on experience, it would be this: *That the pupil be initiated into the translation of the Scriptures, with as little delay as possible.* The Bible is the only rock whence a thorough knowledge of Hebrew can be hewn, and if it be desired that the pupil obtain such knowledge, let him become familiar with the original stock of words contained in that Book. To allow him to spend month after month, and sometimes year after year, in the mere reading of Hebrew, leaving him totally unacquainted with the meaning of what he reads, is as irrational as it is unprofitable. As soon as he is able to read with moderate correctness—

which pupils of ordinary capacity can acquire in a f
months—let him begin to translate; and it will be fou
that his beginning to understand what he reads, w
greatly advance his proficiency in reading, since it is qui
natural that we can with greater facility pronounce wor
which we understand, than those which we can only sp
This method would greatly diminish, if not altogeth
remove, the prolixity and tedium so much complained
in the study of Hebrew. It is proposed that the stude
commit to memory a certain number of nouns, verbs, a
particles, say as many as occur in one chapter, or a p
tion of it, according as his time and capacity will admi
then study the lists of prefixes and suffixes; and, stor
with this preliminary knowledge, let him apply himse
to his Bible, and a very little assistance on the part of t
instructor will soon make him master of the lesson pr
scribed. By proceeding in this course, it has been found th
even small children acquired, in a very short time, an asto
ishing familiarity with the lessons they had gone throug
and it is confidently hoped that the same experience w
be gained by all who apply this book to its proper use.

Notwithstanding the care and attention bestowed upo
this work, we fear that still some errors have crept in, f
which we beg the reader's indulgence. For many a co
rection and kind suggestion we are indebted to the R
S. Morais, who kindly assisted us in revising the work
and we gladly take this opportunity to express our thank
for his gratuitous aid so generously given.

That this book may serve to facilitate the study of th
sacred language, and tend to promote the knowledge o
God's Holy Word, is the sincere wish of

THE AUTHOR.

PHILADELPHIA Kislev, 5625.

CONTENTS.

A SYNOPSIS

OF

HEBREW GRAMMAR.

As the words in this Vocabulary appear mostly in their primitive forms, without affixes, we give here some rules and instructions by which the student may be enabled to understand the construction of each word, with its prefixes and suffixes, and the different uses and import of the same.

It is necessary for him to know, in the first place, how to distinguish the radicals from the servile letters, and next to know the power and meaning of the latter; that of the former being found in the Vocabulary.

It is impossible, however, to give any series of invariable rules by which this distinction can be determined, but the following rules will be found of material assistance in discovering the radicals and serviles of each word distinctively.

§ 1. Nearly every word in the Hebrew language may be reduced to a root of three letters, which are called *radicals;* whereas, those which are added for the purpose of forming tenses, moods, gender, number, person, etc., are called *serviles.* These radicals, how-

(11)

ever, do not always appear in every word, as one is often omitted, and sometimes, though very rarely, two are wanting.

§ 2.   Only eleven letters of the alphabet are used as serviles, viz.: א ב ה ו י כ ל מ נ ת ש, of which, to assist the memory, the words איתן משה וכלב are formed; while the letters א ב ל ש, forming the word אלבש, serve only as prefixes, but the other seven either as prefixes or suffixes. The remaining letters ג ד ז ח ט ס ע פ צ ק ר, making the words גזע צדק טח ספר, are consequently never used as serviles.

§ 3.   It may at the outset be proper to observe, that, with some grammarians, though they constitute, perhaps, the minority, we hold the opinion that the noun, not the verb, forms the principal part of speech, and is entitled to priority. We have, therefore, given it the precedence in the order of the Vocabulary, and shall treat it first here, likewise.

THE NOUN.

§ 4.   Though nouns are, like verbs, derived from abstract roots, yet in the former the radicals do not exert that controlling influence which they do in the latter. In the noun the idea of the root is conceived of as at rest, and unconnected with either person, time, or manner. Nor do the servile letters exercise the same power on the nouns which they do on the verbs; as they are often added to the root, to constitute with it, the noun in its primitive form. Such is the case especially with the letters מ, ת and ה, the latter only at the end; besides the mutes ו and י, which are often inserted without effecting any change in the sense of the word. For the uninitiated it is therefore more difficult, but at the same time less necessary, to distinguish the radicals of nouns, than it is of verbs. To scholars using this Vocabulary it will be sufficient to say, that the nouns appear there in their original forms, and are subject to the prefixes and affixes which here follow with their definitions.

PREFIXES.

§ 5. — הַ with dagesh in the following letter, — הָ or — הֶ without dagesh following, express. the definite article, *the;* as, הַדָּבָר *the* thing, הָאִישׁ *the* man, הֶעָנָן *the* cloud.

— הַ or — הָ without dagesh following, denotes interrogation; as, הַאַתָּה *is it* thou? הֲלֹא *is it* not?

— וּ stands for the copulative *and;* as, אָבִי וְאַחַי וְצֹאנָם וּבְקָרָם, my father, *and* my brothers, *and* their small cattle, *and* their large cattle.

— בְּ stands for *in, with, on,* or other prepositions such as the context may require, as, בְּאֶרֶץ *in* a land, בְּאֶבֶן *with* a stone, בְּהָר *on* a mountain.

— כְּ expresses comparison and proportion gene-

2

rally, and answers to the words *as, like, according to*, etc.; as, כְּעֶבֶד *as* a servant, כְּמֹשֶׁה *like* Moses, כִּדְמוּתֵנוּ *according to* our likeness.

— לְ denotes *to, for*, etc.; as, לְאִישׁ *to* a man, לְשָׁנָה *for* a year.

(When the definite article הַ is to follow either of the prefixes, בְּ, כְּ, לְ, the two are generally abbreviated into, בַּ, כַּ, לַ.)

— מִ or— מֵ means *from, out of*; as, מֵאִישׁ *from* a man, מִגּוֹי *from* a nation, מִגַּן־עֵדֶן *out of* the garden of Eden.

After adjectives it denotes the comparative degree, *more than;* as, מָתוֹק מִדְּבַשׁ *sweet more than*, i. e. sweeter than honey, עַז מֵאֲרִי *stronger than* a lion.

These definitions do not embrace all that the prefixes may imply. Their meaning varies according to what the context may require.

AFFIXES.

§ 6.   הָ — with the accent on the last syllable, denotes the feminine gender; as, אִישׁ *man,* אִשָּׁה *woman,* נָבִיא *prophet,* נְבִיאָה *prophetess.*

הָ — with the accent on the penultimate, is sometimes used to denote *towards* a place:

as, חָרָן Haran, חָרָנָה *towards* Haran, אֶרֶץ
land, אַרְצָה *towards* the land. (Nouns ter-
minating in ה change that letter into ת,
as, מָרָה *Marah,* מָרָתָה *to Marah.*)

ת — with the accent on the penultimate denotes the feminine gender of nouns derived·
from verbs, strictly participles; as אֹמֵן
nurse, f. אֹמֶנֶת·

ים — indicates the plural of masculine nouns;
as, יוֹם *day,* יָמִים *days,* בַּיִת *house,* בָּתִּים
houses.

ים — is used to express two of a kind; as, יַד
hand,־יָדַיִם *two hands,* יוֹם *day,* יוֹמַיִם *two days.*

ות — indicates the plural of feminine nouns;
as, מִצְוָה *command,* מִצְוֹת *commands,* עֲגָלָה
wagon, עֲגָלוֹת *wagons.*

§7. The following affixes are used to denote the
possessive pronouns:

		שִׁיר *a song,* m.		שִׁירָה *a song,* f.
י — my	שִׁירִי *my song,* c.		שִׁירָתִי
ךָ — thy, m.	שִׁירְךָ *thy —,* m.		שִׁירָתֶךָ
ךְ — thy, f.	שִׁירֵךְ *thy —,* f.		שִׁירָתֵךְ
וֹ — his	שִׁירוֹ *his —,*		שִׁירָתוֹ
ה — her	שִׁירָה *her —,*		שִׁירָתָה
נוּ — our	שִׁירֵנוּ *our —,* c.		שִׁירָתֵנוּ
כֶם — your, m.	שִׁירְכֶם *your —,* m.		שִׁירַתְכֶם
כֶן — your, f.	שִׁירְכֶן *your —,* f.		שִׁירַתְכֶן
ם — their, m.	שִׁירָם *their —,* m.		שִׁירָתָם
ן — their, f.	שִׁירָן *their —,* f.		שִׁירָתָן

When the things possessed are plural:

	שִׁירִים songs, m.		שִׁירוֹת songs, f.
־ִי my	שִׁירַי my songs, c.		שִׁירוֹתַי
־ֶיךָ thy, m.	שִׁירֶיךָ thy —, m.		שִׁירוֹתֶיךָ
־ַיִךְ thy, f.	שִׁירַיִךְ thy —, f.		שִׁירוֹתַיִךְ
־ָיו his	שִׁירָיו his —		שִׁירוֹתָיו
־ֶיהָ her	שִׁירֶיהָ her —		שִׁירוֹתֶיהָ
־ֵינוּ our	שִׁירֵינוּ our —, c.		שִׁירוֹתֵינוּ
־ֵיכֶם your, m.	שִׁירֵיכֶם your —, m.		שִׁירוֹתֵיכֶם
־ֵיכֶן your, f.	שִׁירֵיכֶן your —, f.		שִׁירוֹתֵיכֶן
־ֵיהֶם their, m.	שִׁירֵיהֶם their —, m.		שִׁירוֹתֵיהֶם
־ֵיהֶן their, f.	שִׁירֵיהֶן their —, f.		שִׁירוֹתֵיהֶן

When the noun terminates in ה, as, שִׁירָה, תְּפִלָּה,
the same is changed into ת, thus שִׁירָתִי, תְּפִלָּתִי.

To the above list may be added, the terminations
־ִי, ־ִית and ־ָיָה, by which patronimics, or nouns
denoting extraction, are formed from proper names;
as, עִבְרִי *a Hebrew*, f. עִבְרִית, or עִבְרִיָּה, from עֵבֶר
Heber; עַמּוֹנִי *an Ammonite*, f. עַמּוֹנִית, from עַמּוֹן
Ammon.

GENDER.

§ 8.   There are two genders, the masculine and the
feminine. The masculine has properly no distinguishing form, but the groundform of any noun is
naturally to be conceived of as masculine. Accord-
ingly, nouns are for the most part of the masculine
(1) which end in one of the original radicals of the

word; as, רֹאשׁ *head*, בֶּגֶד *garment*, etc. (2) Those ending in הָ—, אֶ—, or אַ—; as, עָלֶה *leaf*, טֶנֶא *basket*, כִּסֵּא *seat*, etc. (3) Those ending in י, ם, or ן; as, פְּרִי *fruit*, יוֹם *day*, תַּנִּין *sea-monster*, etc. (4) The names of nations, rivers, and mountains; and (5) all names of males and their functions.

Of the feminine are: (1) Nouns ending in הָ—, תָ—, תֶ—, ית—, and ות—. (2) The names of countries and cities; and (3) the names of females and their functions.

There is a considerable number of nouns which are used either in the masculine or feminine, and are said to be of the common gender.

NUMBER.

§ 9. Hebrew nouns admit of three numbers — the singular, plural, and dual. Masculine nouns form their plural by the addition of ים—, and feminine nouns by the addition of ות—, to the singular; while the dual is formed by the termination ַיִם—. This rule, however, admits of many exceptions.

PERSON.

§ 10. Nouns have three persons—first, second, and third. The personal pronouns may be found in their regular order on page 106; and the possessive pronominal suffixes on pages 15 and 16.

2*

CASE.

§ 11. The relations of nouns to the verbs with which they are connected, are expressed in Hebrew by the prefixes, מ, ל, כ, ב, or by the prepositions אֶל to, מִן from, and by the particle אֵת; as, עִיר a city, בְּעִיר in a city, כְּעִיר as a city, לְעִיר or אֶל־עִיר to a city, מֵעִיר from a city, or מִן הָעִיר from the city, אֶת הָעִיר the city—the latter denoting the objective case. The relations they bear to other nouns, and the possessive case, are expressed by placing the two words in close connection, which is technically termed *the constructive state*, the words being sometimes connected by a hyphen, thus forming a compound word; as, כְּלִי בַרְזֶל a vessel of iron, or an iron vessel, בֵּית הַמֶּלֶךְ the house of the king, or the king's house, בֶּן־הָגָר son of Hagar. The noun thus defined, or placed in a state of construction, must precede that which defines or qualifies it, and generally suffers a change of vowel. The definite ה, when required, is placed before the word defining, not before that which is defined.

THE VERB.

§ 12. In verbs, the distinction between radicals and serviles, and their respective power, are more particularly to be observed. In order to facilitate the nicer distinctions of the constituent parts of each verb, some particular root is used as a paradigm, or model-verb, to which every other root is compared; and as the verb essentially implies *action*, the verb פָּעַל, *to act*, has been adopted for that purpose, and the radicals of any verb are represented by the three letters, פ ע ל. Thus, for instance, verbs whose first radical is נ, are called the class of פ־נ; those whose middle letter is ו, ע־י; if the last letter is ת, ל־ת, etc.

§ 13. Grammarians have divided the verbs into five classes. The first is called שְׁלֵמִים, *Perfect;* and comprises those verbs in which all the radicals appear throughout every conjugation.

The second class, חֲסֵרִים, *Defective*, comprises verbs whose first radical is נ; some verbs beginning with י; and the verbs לָתַע and לָקַח. These are called *defective* because the first radical is sometimes dropped, and are respectively denominated חֲסְרֵי פ־נ *defective in the first radical, being a* נ; חֲסָר פ־י, *defective in the first radical, being a* י; and חֲסָר פ־ל, *defective in the first radical, being a* ל; besides the verbs ending in נ or ת, which drop the last radical whenever the same letter is added as a pronominal affix. These are termed חֲסְרֵי ל, *defective in the third radical.*

The third class, נָחִים, *Resting*, comprehends roots in which one of the radicals is י or ו, ה, א, and is quiescent. Thus we have roots beginning with א or י, called נְחֵי פ־א and נְחֵי פ־י; roots having ו for the second radical, called נְחֵי ע־ו; and others having

א or ה for the last radical, called נְחֵי לְ־א and
נְחֵי לְ־ה·

The fourth class, כְּפוּלִים, *Doubled*, comprises those
in which the second and third radicals are the same.

And last, מְרֻכָּבִים, *Mixed*, comprising such roots as
partake of the nature of the second and third classes.

§ 14.   Hebrew verbs have seven different forms of
conjugation, technically called בִּנְיָנִים, *buildings* or
constructions.   These represent as many modifications
of the verbal idea, and are as follows:

(1.) קַל or פָּעַל, *Simple active*. This form has no
distinguishing mark, and presents the simple idea of
the verb, free from any modifications except those of
active transitive and intransitive.

(2.) נִפְעַל, *Simple passive*. This form is distinguished by the prefix נ; but when yet another prefix
is required the נ is omitted, and represented by a
dagesh in the first radical.

(3.) פִּעֵל, *Intense active ;* distinguished by *dagesh*
in the second radical.

(4.) פֻּעַל, *Intense passive ;* distinguished by *dagesh*
in the second radical, and — under the first radical.

(5.) הִפְעִיל, *Causative active ;* distinguished by the
prefix ה, and — or יִ— under the second radical.

(6.) הָפְעַל, *Causative passive ;* distinguished by
the prefix ה with short — or — under it.

(7.) הִתְפַּעֵל, *Reflexive ;* characterized by the prefix הִתְ—·

These distinguishing prefixes and other marks, however, do not always appear throughout the conjugations. Sometimes they are represented by a *dagesh*, or the change of a short vowel into a long one, and sometimes there is no compensation at all for them. A thorough acquaintance with the different paradigms of the various classes of verbs only, can enable the student to determine in all cases the exact form of the verb. Nor is the sense of active and passive implied by these forms always strictly so, as their meaning is sometimes differently applied. This is especially the case with the second and seventh forms. Thus, for instance, we have נִשְׁבַּע (in the second form) *to swear*, נִלְחַם *to fight*, etc., and הִתְפַּלֵּל (in the seventh form) *to pray*, הִתְאַנֵּף *to be angry*, etc. Some verbs have quite a different signification in different forms; as, פָּתַח (1st form) *to open*, פִּתַּח (3d form) *to engrave;* while others have in the 3d form a directly opposite or negative meaning; as, סָקַל (1st form) *to stone*, סִקֵּל (3d form) *to remove stones*, דִּשֵּׁן *to remove ashes.*

MOODS.

§ 15. Verbs admit of three moods—the infinitive, the indicative, and the imperative. For the infinitive and imperative we have appropriate forms, as,

שָׁמֹר *to keep,* שְׁמֹר *keep,* הָלֹךְ *to go,* לֵךְ *go,* etc., while the indicative is merged, as it were, in the general species of conjugation. The subjunctive, however, is expressed by a distinct particle, as, אִם *if;* or by the prefix הַ, when it partakes of the interrogative force of that letter, as, הֲיֵלֵךְ בְּתוֹרָתִי אִם לֹא *whether they will walk in my law or not,* הַעוֹדָם חַיִּים *whether they are yet alive;* while the potential is sometimes expressed by the future, as, אֲשֶׁר לֹא תֵעָשֶׂינָה *which ought not to be done,* וְיִכְזָב *that he should lie;* or by an appropriate particle such as אוּלַי *perhaps;* or by some particular verb expressive of that mood, as, יָכֹל *to can,* אָבָה *to will.*

TENSES.

§ 16. The Hebrew has properly but two tenses—the past and the future. The past is formed by subjoining to the ground-form of the conjugation certain pronominal appendages, designating at the same time number, person, and gender, as illustrated in the table on the following page.

The future is formed by prefixing to the ground-form the letters נ, ת, י, א, and affixing וּ to the second and third pers. pl. masc., and הָ— to the fem., with such vowel-changes as the forms respectively require.

PARADIGM OF A PERFECT VERB IN THE FIRST CONJUGATION.

Infinitive mood פְּקֹד *to visit.*

With the prepositions בִּפְקֹד *in visiting,* כִּפְקֹד *as visiting,* לִפְקֹד *(in order) to visit,* מִפְּקֹד *from visiting.*

Imperative mood פְּקֹד masc. sing., פִּקְדִי fem. sing., פִּקְדוּ masc. pl., פְּקֹדְנָה fem. pl.

	FUTURE.		PAST.	
	Masculine.	Feminine.	Feminine.	Masculine.
I.	אֶפְקֹד	אֶפְקֹד	פָּקַדְתִּי	פָּקַדְתִּי
thou.	תִּפְקֹד	תִּפְקְדִי	פָּקַדְתְּ	פָּקַדְתָּ
he.	יִפְקֹד	תִּפְקֹד	פָּקְדָה	פָּקַד
we.	נִפְקֹד	נִפְקֹד	פָּקַדְנוּ	פָּקַדְנוּ
ye.	תִּפְקְדוּ	תִּפְקֹדְנָה	פְּקַדְתֶּן	פְּקַדְתֶּם
they.	יִפְקְדוּ	תִּפְקֹדְנָה	פָּקְדוּ	פָּקְדוּ

Participle active used with the pronouns for the present.	
פֹּקֵד m.	
פֹּקֶדֶת f.	
פֹּקְדִים m. pl.	
פֹּקְדוֹת f. pl.	

Participle passive used with the pronouns for the present.	
פָּקוּד m.	
פְּקוּדָה f.	
פְּקוּדִים m. pl.	
פְּקוּדוֹת f. pl.	

As this table is intended merely to illustrate the formation of the tenses by means of the pronominal affixes, we have given only a paradigm of the קַל, according to the analogy of which the other conjugations, and even the other classes of verbs, more or less proceed.

The present is expressed generally by using the participle, as, דֹּבֵר אָנֹכִי *I am speaking*, אַתָּה יוֹשֵׁב *thou art sitting*, הוּא הֹלֵךְ *he is going*—AM, ART, and IS being understood, but never expressed.

The tenses and the participles, however, are used rather indiscriminately, examples of which may be found in Gen. xxii. 12, xlviii. 6; Ex. xviii. 15; Num. ix. 16; Deut. v. 5; and numerous other places.

The prefix וֹ besides being used as a copulative, has the power of changing the tense, and is then called the וֹ *conversive*. When changing future into past, it is וָ or וַ, as, אֹמַר *I will say*, וָאֹמַר *and I said*, יֵלֵךְ *he will go*, וַיֵּלֶךְ *and he went;* when changing past into future, וֹ or וְ, as, מָדְדוּ *they measured*, וּמָדְדוּ *and they shall measure*, אָמְרוּ *they said*, וְאָמְרוּ *and they shall say*.

ADJECTIVES.

§ 17. In Hebrew grammar, adjectives belong properly to the class of nouns, and are termed שְׁמוֹת הַתֹּאַר *Nouns of quality*, or *Qualifying nouns*. As such they admit of number and gender, in which they agree with the nouns they qualify; thus:

אִישׁ טוֹב *a good man.* אֲנָשִׁים טוֹבִים *good men.*
אִשָּׁה טוֹבָה *a good woman,* נָשִׁים טוֹבוֹת *good women.*

Adjectives are usually placed after their respective nouns, as above. Sometimes, however, they are placed before the noun, when they cease to be the qualifying word, and become the predicate of the noun which they accompany, as, עֲוֹנִי גָּדוֹל *my sin is great,* טוֹב אֲדֹנָי *the Lord is good.*

When a noun is in a definite state, having the definite ה, or any of the pronominal affixes, the adjective receives the definite ה likewise, otherwise it is also a predicate, as, הָאִישׁ הַטּוֹב *the good man,* בְּנוֹ הַקָּטָן, *his youngest son;* but הָאִישׁ טוֹב *the man is good,* בְּנוֹ קָטָן *his son is young.*

DEGREES OF COMPARISON.

§ 18. The comparative degree is expressed by prefixing מ to the noun. (See list of prefixes.)

The superlative degree is marked by prefixing ה to the adjective, and בּ to the following noun, as, הַיָּפָה בַּנָּשִׁים *the fairest among women,* or, if the noun precedes and is defined, by placing ה before the adjective, as, אָחִיו הַגָּדוֹל *his eldest brother.*

As the numerals, pronouns, and other parts of speech included by ancient grammarians under the class of particles, are of minor consideration, and, as far as they occur in the Pentateuch, are given in the Vocabulary, it is not deemed necessary to treat of them in this limited treatise. .

3

For the accommodation of juvenile scholars, we add this list of prefixes and affixes, with their definitions abbreviated.

PREFIXES.

— הַ stands for *the*, or *is it?*

— וְ   "   "   *and.*

— בְּ   "   "   *in, with, on*, etc.

— כְּ   "   "   *as, like*, etc.

— לְ   "   "   *to, for*, etc.

— מִ   "   "   *from, out of*, etc.

AFFIXES.

ה ָ denotes the feminine gender, or, *towards.*

ת ֶ   "   the feminine gender of participles.

ים ִ   "   the plural of masculine nouns.

ִם ַ   "   two of a kind.

וֹת —   "   the plural of feminine nouns.

A VOCABULARY

THE PENTATEUCH.

(27)

NOUNS.

GENESIS.

בְּרֵאשִׁית

Beginning. Firstling.	רֵאשִׁית
God. Judges.[1]	אֱלֹהִים
Heaven.	שָׁמַיִם
Earth. Land.	אֶרֶץ
Darkness.	חֹשֶׁךְ
Face. Surface.	פָּנִים
Abyss.	תְּהוֹם
Spirit. Wind. Breath.[2]	רוּחַ
Water.	מַיִם
Light.	אוֹר
Day.	יוֹם
Night.	לַיְלָה
Evening.	עֶרֶב
Morning.	בֹּקֶר
Firmament.	רָקִיעַ
Midst.	תָּוֶךְ
Place.	מָקוֹם
The dry land.	יַבָּשָׁה
Gathering.	מִקְוֶה
Sea. The West.	יָם
Grass.	דֶּשֶׁא
Herbage.	עֵשֶׂב
Seed. Offspring.	זֶרַע
Tree. Wood. Gallows.[1]	עֵץ
Fruit.	פְּרִי
Kind.	מִין
Luminary.	מָאוֹר
Sign.	אוֹת
Season. Feast. Assembly.[2]	מוֹעֵד
Year.	שָׁנָה
Rule.	מֶמְשָׁלָה
Star.	כּוֹכָב
Reptile.	שֶׁרֶץ

---

[1] Ex. 21: 6.   [2] Ex. 15: 8.   [1] Deut. 21: 22.   [2] Num. 16: 2.

Soul. Life. Person.[1] Corpse.[2] Mind.[3]	נֶפֶשׁ	Plant.	שִׂיחַ
Fowl.	עוֹף	Field.	שָׂדֶה
Sea-monster. Serpent.[4]	תַּנִּין	Mist.	אֵד
Wing. Skirt.[5] Extremity[6] (of a garment).	כָּנָף	Dust. Mortar.[1]	עָפָר
Cattle. Beast.	בְּהֵמָה	Nostrils. Face. Anger.	אַפַּיִם
Creeping animals.	רֶמֶשׂ	Breath. Soul.	נְשָׁמָה
Animal.	חַיָּה	Life.	חַיִּים
Earth. Land.	אֲדָמָה	Garden.	גַּן
Man (human being).	אָדָם	The East. Antiquity.[2]	קֶדֶם
Image.	צֶלֶם	Sight. Appearance.	מַרְאֶה
Likeness.	דְּמוּת	Food.	מַאֲכָל
Fish.	דָּגָה	Knowledge.	דַּעַת
All. The whole.	כֹּל	Good.	טוֹב
Male.	זָכָר	Evil.	רַע
Female.	נְקֵבָה	River.	נָהָר
Food.	אָכְלָה	Head. Beginning. Poison.[3]	רֹאשׁ
Greenness.	יָרָק	Name.	שֵׁם

CHAP. 2

Host. Army.	צָבָא	Gold.	זָהָב
Labor. Property.[7]	מְלָאכָה	Bdellium.	בְּדֹלַח
History. Generation.	תּוֹלְדוֹת	Stone.	אֶבֶן
		Onyx.	שֹׁהַם
		Help.	עֵזֶר
		A deep sleep.	תַּרְדֵּמָה

[1] Ex. 1: 5.   [2] Lev. 21: 11.   [3] Gen. 23: 8.
[4] Ex. 7: 9.   [5] Deut. 23: 1.   [6] Num. 15: 38.
[7] Ex. 22: 7.

[1] Lev. 14: 42   [2] Deut. 33: 27.   [3] Deut. 32: 33.

Rib. Side.[1]	צֵלָע	Thorn.	קוֹץ
Flesh.	בָּשָׂר	Thistle.	דַּרְדַּר
Woman. Wife.	אִשָּׁה	Sweat.	זֵעָה
Time. Corner.[2]	פַּעַם	Bread. Food.	לֶחֶם
Bone.	עֶצֶם	Living being.	חַי
Man. Husband.	אִישׁ	Coat.	כֻּתֹּנֶת
Father. Originator.[3]	אָב	Skin. Hide.	עוֹר
Mother.	אֵם	Hand. Power. Side. Portion.	יָד

CHAP. 3.

Serpent.	נָחָשׁ	Cherub.	כְּרוּב
Eye. Spring. Appearance.[4]	עַיִן	Flame.	לַהַט
Desire. Boundary.[5]	תַּאֲוָה	Sword. A sharp instrument.[1] Drought.[2]	חֶרֶב
Leaf.	עָלֶה	Way. Manner.[3] Journey.[4]	דֶּרֶךְ
Fig. Fig-tree.	תְּאֵנָה		

CHAP. 4.

Girdle. Apron.	חֲגוֹרָה	Brother. Kinsman.[5]	אָח
Voice.	קוֹל	Shepherd.	רֹעֶה
Belly.	גָּחוֹן	Small cattle.	צֹאן
Enmity.	אֵיבָה	End..	קֵץ
Heel. Rear.[6]	עָקֵב	Offering. Present.	מִנְחָה
Pain. Toil.	עִצָּבוֹן	Firstling. First-born.	בְּכוֹר
Pregnancy.	הֵרֹן	Fat. The choicest part.[6]	חֵלֶב
Pain. Toil.	עֶצֶב	Elevation. A swelling.[7]	שְׂאֵת
Desire.	תְּשׁוּקָה		

---

[1] Ex. 26: 26.   [2] Ex. 25: 12.   [3] Gen. 4: 20, 21.   [4] Lev. 13: 55.   [5] Gen. 49: 26.   [6] Gen. 49: 19.

[1] Ex. 20: 25.   [2] Deut. 28: 22.   [3] Gen. 19: 31.   [4] Num. 11: 31.   [5] Gen. 29: 15.   [6] Num. 18: 1.   [7] Lev. 13: 2.

Entrance. Opening.	פֶּתַח
Sin. Sin-offering.	חַטָּאת
Keeper.	שֹׁמֵר
Blood. Guilt.[1]	דָּם
Mouth. Command.[2] Edge.[3] Portion.[4]	פֶּה
Strength. Chameleon.[5]	כֹּחַ
Sin.	עָוֹן
City.	עִיר
Son. Child.	בֵּן
Women. Wives.	נָשִׁים
Tent.	אֹהֶל
Cattle. Purchase.[6]	מִקְנֶה
Harp.	כִּנּוֹר
Reed-pipe.	עוּגָב
Instrument.	חֶרֶשׁ
Copper.	נְחֹשֶׁת
Iron.	בַּרְזֶל
Sister.	אָחוֹת
Speech. Word.	אִמְרָה
Wound.	פֶּצַע
Child.	יֶלֶד
Bruise.	חַבֻּרָה

CHAP. 5.

| Book. Writing.[1] | סֵפֶר |

CHAP. 6.

Daughter.	בַּת
Deed. Work.	מַעֲשֶׂה
Perpetual time. Olden time.	עוֹלָם
Giants.	נְפִלִים
Hero. Chief.	גִּבּוֹר
Man.	אֱנוֹשׁ
Evil.	רָעָה
Propensity.	יֵצֶר
Thought.	מַחֲשָׁבָה
Heart. Midst.	לֵב
Grace.	חֵן

נח

Generation.	דּוֹר
Violence.	חָמָס
Ark. Chest.	תֵּבָה
Gopher (a kind of wood).	גֹּפֶר
Kennel. Nest.	קֵן
House. Household. Inner-part.	בַּיִת
The outside.	חוּץ

---

[1] Numb. 35: 27. [2] Gen. 45: 21. [3] Deut. 20: 13. [4] Deut. 21: 17. [5] Lev. 11: 30. [6] Gen. 49: 32.

[1] Deut. 24: 1.

Pitch. Ransom.[1]	כֹּפֶר	Palm of the hand. Hand. Sole of the foot. Bowl.[1] Branch.[2]	כַּף
Cubit.	אַמָּה		
Length.	אֹרֶךְ	Foot. Pace.[3]	רֶגֶל
Breadth.	רֹחַב	Time.	עֵת
Height.	קוֹמָה	Olive. Olive-tree.	זַיִת
Light.	צֹהַר	Covering.	מִכְסֶה
Side.	צַד	Family.	מִשְׁפָּחָה
Deluge.	מַבּוּל	Altar.	מִזְבֵּחַ
Covenant.	בְּרִית	Burnt-offering.	עֹ לָה

CHAP. 7.

Living creature.	יְקוּם	Smell.	רֵיחַ
Month. New-moon's day.[2]	חֹדֶשׁ	Youth.	נְעוּרִים
Fountain.	מַעְיָן	Harvest-time.	קָצִיר
Window.	אֲרֻבָּה	Cold.	קֹר
Rain.	גֶּשֶׁם	Heat.	חֹם
Bird.	צִפּוֹר	Summer.	קַיִץ
Mountain.	הַר	Winter. Autumn.	חֹרֶף
Dry Land.	חָרָבָה		

CHAP. 8.

CHAP. 9.

Window.	חַלּוֹן	Fear. A fearful act.[4]	מוֹרָא
Raven.	עֹרֵב	Dread.	חִתָּה
Dove.	יוֹנָה	Fish.	דָּג
Resting-place.	מָנוֹחַ	Bow.	קֶשֶׁת
		Cloud.	עָנָן

---

[1] Ex. 21: 30.   [2] Num. 29: 6.

[1] Ex. 25: 29.   [2] Lev. 23: 40.   [3] Gen. 33: 14.   [4] Deut. 4: 34.

Vineyard.	כֶּרֶם	Mortar. Heap.[1] Homer (A measure).	חֹמֶר
Wine.	יַיִן	Tower.	מִגְדָּל
Nakedness. Shame.[1]	עֶרְוָה	People.	עַם
Garment.	שִׂמְלָה	Nativity. Progeny.[2] Birth-place.[3]	מוֹלֶדֶת
Shoulder. Portion.[2]	שְׁכֶם	Child.	וְלֶד
Servant.	עֶבֶד	Daughter-in-law.	כַּלָּה

CHAP. 10.

CHAP. 12.

לֵךְ לְךָ

Island. Coast.	אִי	Blessing. Present.[4]	בְּרָכָה
Nation.	גּוֹי	Substance. Wealth.	רְכוּשׁ
Tongue. Language.	לָשׁוֹן	Oak. Grove.	אֵלוֹן
Hunting. Venison.	צַיִד	The South.	נֶגֶב
Kingdom.	מַמְלָכָה	Hunger. Famine.	רָעָב
Boundary.	גְּבוּל	Prince. Chief.	שַׂר
Seat. Dwelling.	מוֹשָׁב	Cattle.	בָּקָר

CHAP. 11.

Lip. Language. Border.	שָׂפָה	Ass.	חֲמוֹר
Word. Thing.	דָּבָר	Bond-woman.	שִׁפְחָה
Valley.	בִּקְעָה	She-ass.	אָתוֹן
Friend. Fellow-being. Shouting.[3]	רֵעַ	Camel.	גָּמָל
Brick.	לְבֵנָה	Plague. Stroke.[5]	נֶגַע
Burning.	שְׂרֵפָה		
Slime.	חֵמָר		

CHAP. 13.

Silver. Money.	כֶּסֶף
Journey.	מַסַּע

---

[1] Deut. 23: 15   [2] Gen. 48: 22.   [3] Ex. 32: 17.

[1] Ex. 8: 10.   [2] Gen. 48: 6.   [3] Gen 31: 3.   [4] Gen. 33: 11.   [5] Deut. 17. 6.

Strife.	רִיב / מְרִיבָה
Left hand. Left side.	שְׂמֹאל
Right hand. Right side.	יָמִין
Plain. Cake.[1] Talent.[2]	כִּכָּר
Sinners.	חַטָּאִים
The North	צָפוֹן

CHAP. 14.

King.	מֶלֶךְ
War.	מִלְחָמָה
Valley.	עֵמֶק
Salt.	מֶלַח
Desert.	מִדְבָּר
Pit. Well.	בְּאֵר
Food. Eating.[3]	אֹכֶל
One who escaped.	פָּלִיט
Master. Husband.	בַּעַל
Confederate.	בַּעַל בְּרִית
One who is initiated.	חָנִיךְ
Native. Descendant.[4]	יָלִיד
Priest.	כֹּהֵן
God. Might.[5]	אֵל
Enemy. Distress.[6]	צָר

[1] Ex. 29: 23. [2] Ex. 38: 25. [3] Ex. 12: 4. [4] Nu. 13: 32. [5] Gen. 31: 29. [6] Deut. 4: 30.

Tithe.	מַעֲשֵׂר
Thread. Line.	חוּט
Latchet.	שְׂרוֹךְ
Shoe.	נַעַל
Portion.	חֵלֶק

CHAP. 15.

Vision.	מַחֲזֶה
Shield.	מָגֵן
Reward.	שָׂכָר
Steward.	בֶּן־מֶשֶׁק
Bowels. Entrails.	מֵעַיִם
Righteousness.	צְדָקָה
Calf. Heifer.	עֶגְלָה
Goat.	עֵז
Ram.	אַיִל
Turtledove.	תּוֹר
A young bird.	גּוֹזָל
Piece.	בֶּתֶר
Bird of prey.	עַיִט
Carcass.	פֶּגֶר
Sun.	שֶׁמֶשׁ
Terror.	אֵימָה
Darkness.	חֲשֵׁכָה
Stranger.	גֵּר
Peace. Welfare.	שָׁלוֹם

Old age. Hoariness.	שֵׂיבָה
Thick darkness.	עֲלָטָה
Furnace. Oven.	תַּנּוּר
Smoke.	עָשָׁן
Flame.	לַפִּיד
Fire.	אֵשׁ
Piece. Part.	גְּזֶר

CHAP. 16.

Mistress.	גְּבֶרֶת
Bosom. Lap.	חֵיק
Messenger. Angel.	מַלְאָךְ
Multitude.	רֹב
Wretchedness. Poverty.	עֳנִי
Wild ass.	פֶּרֶא

CHAP. 17.

The Almighty.	שַׁדַּי
Multitude.	הָמוֹן
Sojourn.	מָגוּר
Possession.	אֲחֻזָּה
Foreskin.	עָרְלָה
Possession. Purchase. Price.[1]	מִקְנָה
Stranger.	נֵכָר
One who is uncircumcised.	עָרֵל
Prince.	נָשִׂיא

Lord. Master.	אָדוֹן
A little.	מְעַט
Morsel.	פַּת
Seah (a measure).	סְאָה
Meal.	קֶמַח
Fine flour.	סֹלֶת
Cake.	עֻגָּה
Boy. Young man.	נַעַר
Cream.	חֶמְאָה
Milk.	חָלָב
Manner. Path.	אֹרַח
Midst. Entrails.	קֶרֶב
Pleasure.	עֶדְנָה
Judgment. Justice. Manner. Law.	מִשְׁפָּט
Cry.	זְעָקָה ‏{ צְעָקָה
Destruction.	כָּלָה
A righteous man.	צַדִּיק
A wicked man.	רָשָׁע
Judge.	שֹׁפֵט
Ashes.	אֵפֶר

---

[1] Lev. 25: 16.

CHAP. 19.

Gate. Measure.[1]	שַׁעַר
Street. Square.	רְחוֹב
Repast.	מִשְׁתֶּה
Unleavened bread.	מַצָּה
End.	קָצֶה
Door.	דֶּלֶת
Shadow.	צֵל
Beam.	קֹרָה
Blindness.	סַנְוֵרִים
Son-in-law. Bridegroom.	חָתָן
Dawn.	שַׁחַר
Favor. Mercy. Disgrace.[2]	חֶסֶד
Sulphur.	גָּפְרִית
Inhabitant.	יֹשֵׁב
Growth. Sprout.	צֶמַח
Statue.	נְצִיב
Smoke. Vapor.	קִיטֹר
Kiln.	כִּבְשָׁן
Overthrow.	הֲפֵכָה
Cave.	מְעָרָה
The morrow. The next day.	{ מָחָר מָחֳרָת }
Yesternight.	אֶמֶשׁ

CHAP. 20.

Dream.	חֲלוֹם
Integrity.	תֹּם
Purity.	נִקָּיוֹן
Heart.	לֵכָב
Prophet.	נָבִיא
Ear.	אֹזֶן
Sin.	חֲטָאָה
Fear.	יִרְאָה
Covering. Raiment.[1]	כְּסוּת
Maid-servant.	אָמָה
Womb.	רֶחֶם

CHAP. 21.

Old age.	זְקוּנִים
Laughter.	צְחֹק
Leather bag.	חֵמֶת
Shot.	טַחֲוֶה
Archer.	קַשָּׁת
Immediate offspring.	נִין
Remote progeny.	נֶכֶד
Ewe lamb.	כִּבְשָׂה
Testimony. Assembly.	עֵדָה
Grove.	אֵשֶׁל

---

[1] Gen. 26: 12.   [2] Lev. 20: 17.   [1] Ex. 21: 10.

4

CHAP. 22.		Drinking-trough.	שֹׁקֶת
Butcher's knife.	מַאֲכֶלֶת	Nose-ring. Ear-ring.	נֶזֶם
Sheep. Goat.	שֶׂה	Beka (a weight).	בֶּקַע
Aught.	מְאוּמָה	Weight.	מִשְׁקָל
Thicket.	סְבַךְ	Bracelet. Lid.[1]	צָמִיד
Horn.	קֶרֶן	Straw. ●	תֶּבֶן
Sand.	חוֹל	Provender.	מִסְפּוֹא
Enemy.	אֹיֵב	Truth. Fidelity.	אֱמֶת
Concubine.	פִּילֶגֶשׁ	Old age.	זִקְנָה
CHAP. 23.		Oath. Curse.	אָלָה
חיי שרה		Young woman.	עַלְמָה
Corpse.	מֵת	Vessel. Tool. Ornament. Instrument.	כְּלִי
Sojourner.	תּוֹשָׁב		
Grave.	קֶבֶר	Garment. Covering.	בֶּגֶד
Choice part.	מִבְחַר	Precious things.	מִגְדָּנֹת
Shekel (a weight).	שֶׁקֶל	Nurse.	מֵנֶקֶת
Merchant.	סֹחֵר	Enemy.	שֹׂנֵא
CHAP. 24.		Vail.	צָעִיף
Elder.	זָקֵן		
Thigh. Side.[1] Shaft.[2]	יָרֵךְ	CHAP. 25.	
Oath.	שְׁבוּעָה	Gift.	מַתָּנָה
Wealth. Goodness.	טוּב	The East.	קֶדֶם
Girl. Damsel.	נַעֲרָה	Court. Village.	חָצֵר
Bucket. Jar.	כַּד	Stronghold.	טִירָה
Virgin.	בְּתוּלָה	Nation.	אֻמָּה

תולדות

Belly. Womb.	בֶּטֶן
Nation.	לְאֹם
Twins.	תּוֹמִים
Cloak.	אַדֶּרֶת
Hair.	שֵׂעָר
Pottage.	נָזִיד
Birth-right.	בְּכוֹרָה
Lentiles.	עֲדָשִׁים

CHAP. 26.

Charge. Watch.	מִשְׁמֶרֶת
Commandment.	מִצְוָה
Statute. Allotment.¹	חֹק
Law. Instruction.	תּוֹרָה
Guilt. Trespass-offering. Debt.²	אָשָׁם
Suit of servants.	עֲבֹדָה
Valley. Stream.	נַחַל
Companion.	מֵרֵעַ
Bitterness.	מָרָה

CHAP. 27.

Quiver.	תְּלִי
Savory meats.	מַטְעַמִּים
Kid.	גְּדִי

Impostor.	מְתַעְתֵּעַ
Curse. Contempt.¹	קְלָלָה
Smoothness. Portion.²	חֶלְקָה
Neck.	צַוָּאר
Dew.	טַל
Fatness.	מִשְׁמָן
Corn.	דָּגָן
New wine.	תִּירֹשׁ
Master.	גְּבִיר
Trembling.	חֲרָדָה
Fraud. Subtlety.	מִרְמָה
Yoke	עֹל
Mourning.	אֵבֶל
Anger. Poison.³	חֵמָה
Anger. Nose.	אַף

CHAP. 28.

Assembly.	קָהָל

ויצא

The place where one rests his head.	מְרַאֲשׁוֹת
Ladder.	סֻלָּם
Sleep.	שֵׁנָה
Monument. Statue.	מַצֵּבָה

---

¹ Gen. 47: 22; Ex. 5: 14. ² Num. 5: 7.

¹ Deut. 21: 23. ² Gen. 33: 19. ³ Deut. 32: 24.

40 NOUNS.

Oil.	שֶׁמֶן	Hazel.	לוּז
Vow. Anything vowed.[1]	נֶדֶר	Chestnut.	עַרְמוֹן
CHAP. 29.		Streaks.	פְּצָלוֹת
Flock.	עֵדֶר	Gutter.	רַהַט
Shepherdess.	רֹעָה	**CHAP. 31.**	
Report.	שֵׁמַע	Honor. Glory. Wealth.	כָּבוֹד
Reward.	מַשְׂכֹּרֶת	Yesterday.	תְּמוֹל
Love.	אַהֲבָה	Times.	מֹנִים
Form.	תֹּאַר	Rams.	עַתּוּדִים
A week. Seven years.	שָׁבוּעַ	Inheritance.	נַחֲלָה
Work. Service.	עֲבֹדָה	Stranger.	נָכְרִי
CHAP. 30.		Riches.	עֹשֶׁר
Knee.	בֶּרֶךְ	Acquisition.	קִנְיָן
Wrestlings.	נַפְתּוּלִים	Idolatrous images.	תְּרָפִים
Fortune.	גָּד	Joy.	שִׂמְחָה
Happiness.	אֹשֶׁר	Song.	שִׁיר
Wheat.	חִטִּים	Timbrel.	תֹּף
Mandrakes.	דּוּדָאִים	Saddle-cushion. A fat lamb.[1]	כַּר
Gift.	זֶכֶר	Trespass.	פֶּשַׁע
Reproach.	חֶרְפָּה	Ewe. Sheep.	רָחֵל
Lamb.	כֶּשֶׂב	That which is torn by a wild beast.	טְרֵפָה
He-goat.	תַּיִשׁ	Heat. Drought.	חֹרֶב
Rod.	מַקֵּל	Frost. Ice.	קֶרַח
Poplar.	לִבְנֶה		

[1] Deut. 12: 6.   [1] Deut. 32: 14.

Fear.	פַּחַד	A slain person.	חָלָל
Labor.	יָגִיעַ	Wealth. Power. Host. Valor.	חַיִל
Witness.	עֵד	Little children.	טַף
Heap.	גַּל	Men.	מְתִים
Slaughtering. Sacrifice.	זֶבַח	Number.	מִסְפָּר

CHAP. 32.

Camp. Host.	מַחֲנֶה	Harlot.	זוֹנָה

וישלח

CHAP. 35.

Ox.	שׁוֹר	Distress.	צָרָה
Escape. Residue.	פְּלֵיטָה	Oak.	אֵלָה / אַלּוֹן
Cow.	פָּרָה		
Bull.	פַּר	Loins.	חֲלָצַיִם
A young ass.	עַיִר	Drink-offering.	נֶסֶךְ
Space.	רֶוַח	A long distance.	כִּבְרָה
Passage.	מַעֲבָר	Midwife.	מְיַלֶּדֶת
Sinew.	גִּיד	Grave. Burial-place.	קְבוּרָה

CHAP. 33.

CHAP. 36.

Enough. Much.	רַב	Chief.	אַלּוּף
A slow progress.	אַט	Mules.	יֵמִם
Booth.	סֻכָּה		

CHAP. 37.

Kesitah (a certain weight or coin).	קְשִׂיטָה		

וישב

CHAP. 34.

Girl.	יַלְדָּה	Evil report.	דִּבָּה
A shameful act.	נְבָלָה	Flaps.	פַּסִּים
Marriage price.	מֹהַר	Sheaf.	אֲלֻמָּה
Gift.	מַתָּן	Moon.	יָרֵחַ
		Pit. Prison.	בּוֹר

4*

Caravan.	אֹרְחָה	Scarlet.	שָׁנִי
Spicery.	נְכֹאת	Breach.	פֶּרֶץ

CHAP. 39.

Balm.	צֱרִי	Prison.	סֹהַר
Ladanum.	לֹט	Prisoner.	אָסִיר

Profit. Lucre.	בֶּצַע

CHAP. 40.

He-goat. Satyr.[1] Shower.[2]	שָׂעִיר	Butler. Drink.	מַשְׁקֶה
		Baker.	אֹפֶה
Sack.	שַׂק	Custody. Charge.	מִשְׁמָר
Loins.	מָתְנַיִם	Interpretation.	פִּתְרוֹן
Grave. Hell.	שְׁאוֹל	Vine.	גֶּפֶן
Officer. Eunuch.	סָרִיס	Tendrils.	שָׂרִיגִים
Executioner.	טַבָּח	Blossom. Hawk.[1]	נֵץ

CHAP. 38.

Widow.	אַלְמָנָה	Cluster.	אֶשְׁכֹּל
Father-in-law.	חָם	Grapes.	עֵנָב.עֲנָבִים
Widowhood.	אַלְמָנוּת	Cup. Little owl.[2]	כּוֹס
Pledge.	עֵרָבוֹן	Station. Base.[3]	כֵּן
Signet.	חוֹתָם ,חֹתֶמֶת	Basket.	סַל
String. Thread.	פָּתִיל	White bread.	חֹרִי

CHAP. 41.

מִקֵּץ

Staff. Tribe.	מַטֶּה	River.	יְאֹר
Prostitute.	קְדֵשָׁה	Marsh-grass.	אָחוּ
Disgrace.	בּוּז	Ear of corn.	שִׁבֹּלֶת
Prostitution.	זְנוּנִים	Stalk. Cane. Reed.	קָנֶה
Twins.	תְאוֹמִים		

---

[1] Lev. 17: 7.   [2] Deut. 32: 2.

[1] Lev. 11: 16.   [2] Lev. 11: 17.   [3] Ex. 30: 18.

East wind.	קָדִים
Hieroglyphists.	חַרְטֻמִּים
A wise man.	חָכָם
Sin.	חֵטְא
Badness.	רֹעַ
Beginning.	תְּחִלָּה
Satiety. Plenty.	שָׂבָע
Overseer.	פָּקִיד
Corn.	בַּר
Deposit.	פִּקָּדוֹן
Throne. Seat.	כִּסֵּא
Ring.	טַבַּעַת
Fine linen.	שֵׁשׁ
Collar.	רָבִיד
Chariot.	מֶרְכָּבָה
Handful.	קֹמֶץ
Toil.	עָמָל

CHAP. 42.

Grain. Breach.	שֶׁבֶר
Mischief.	אָסוֹן
Governor.	שַׁלִּיט
Spies.	מְרַגְּלִים
Hunger.	רְעָבוֹן
Interpreter.	מֵלִיץ
Provision.	צֵדָה

Lodging-place.	מָלוֹן
Sack.	אַמְתַּחַת
Bundle.	צְרוֹר
Sorrow.	יָגוֹן

CHAP., 43.

Excellent fruit.	זִמְרָה
Honey.	דְּבַשׁ
Pistacia nuts.	בָּטְנִים
Almonds.	שְׁקֵדִים
Error.	מִשְׁגֶּה
Mercy.	רַחֲמִים
Slaughtering. Cattle to be slaughtered.	טֶבַח
Noon.	צָהֳרַיִם
Treasure.	מַטְמוֹן
Chamber.	חֶדֶר
Abomination.	תּוֹעֵבָה
Youth.	צְעִירָה
Present.	מִשְׁאֵת

CHAP. 44.

Cup.	גָּבִיעַ
Good.	טוֹבָה

CHAP. 45.

וַיִּגַּשׁ

Weeping.	בְּכִי
Sustenance. Healing.[1]	מִחְיָה

---
1 Lev. 13: 10.

Plowing.	חָרִישׁ	Power.	עֹז
Remainder.	שְׁאֵרִית	Rashness.	פַּחַז
Ruler. Poet.[1]	מֹשֵׁל	Bed. Couch. Lying down.[1]	מִשְׁכָּב
Beasts.	בְּעִיר		
Wagon.	עֲגָלָה	Bed. Couch.	יָצוּעַ
Change.	חֲלִיפָה	Sword. Relationship.	מְכֵרָה
		Secret. Counsel.	סוֹד
Food.	מָזוֹן	Will. Favor.	רָצוֹן
Vision.	מַרְאָה	Anger.	עֶבְרָה

CПAP. 47.

End. Portion.	מִקְצֶה	Neck.	עֹרֶף
Pasture.	מִרְעֶה	Whelp (of a lion).	גוּר
The best part.	מֵיטַב	Lion.	אַרְיֵה
Horse.	סוּס	Prey. Food.	טֶרֶף
Body.	גְּוִיָּה	Lioness.	לָבִיא
Product.	תְּבוּאָה	Sceptre. Rod. Tribe.	שֵׁבֶט
A fifth part.	{ חֲמִישִׁית חֹמֶשׁ	Law-giver.	מְחֹקֵק
		Obedience.	יְקֵהָה
וִיחִי			
Bed.	מִטָּה	A choice vine.	שֹׂרֵקָה

CПAP. 48.

Old age.	זָקֵן	Son. The young (of an animal).	בְּנִי
Multitude. Fulness.	מְלֹא	Garment.	{ לְבֻשׁ סוּת

CHAP. 49.

The latter part.	אַחֲרִית	Tooth.	שֵׁן
Strength.	אוֹן	Haven.	חוֹף
Excellence. Residue.[2]	יֶתֶר	Ship.	אֳנִיָּה

Border. Extremity.	יַרְכָה	Progenitors.	הוֹרִים
Bone.	גֶּרֶם	Hill.	גִּבְעָה
Folds.	מִשְׁפְּתָיִם	Crown of the head.	קָדְקֹד
Rest. Resting-place.[1]	מְנוּחָה	One who is separated, or consecrated. An undressed vine.[1]	נָזִיר
Tribute.	מַס		
Adder.	שְׁפִיפוֹן	Wolf.	זְאֵב
Rider.	רֹכֵב	Prey.	עַד
Salvation.	יְשׁוּעָה	Spoil.	שָׁלָל
Troop.	גְּדוּד	CHAP. 50.	
		Physician.	רֹפֵא
Dainties.	מַעֲדַנִּים	Embalming.	חֲנָטִים
Hind.	אַיָּלָה	Weeping.	בְּכִית
Word. Saying.	אֹמֶר	Chariot. The upper mill-stone.[2]	רֶכֶב
Beauty.	שֶׁפֶר		
Wall.	שׁוּר	Horseman.	פָּרָשׁ
Arrow.	חֵץ	Threshing-floor.	גֹּרֶן
Strength.	אֵיתָן	Hawthorn.	אָטָד
Arm. Shin[2] (of cattle).	זְרֹעַ	Side. The opposite.	עֵבֶר
A mighty one.	אַבִּיר	Lamentation.	מִסְפֵּד
Breasts.	שָׁדַיִם	Descendants of the third generation.	שִׁלֵּשִׁים
Womb.	רַחַם	Chest. Ark.	אָרֹן

EXODUS.

שמות

Burden	סִבְלוֹת
Storehouses.	מִסְכְּנוֹת
Rigor.	פֶּרֶךְ
Birth-stool.	אָבְנָיִם

CHAP. 2.

Month.	יֶרַח
Bulrush.	גֹּמֶא
Pitch.	זֶפֶת
Flag (a weed).	סוּף
Cry.	שַׁוְעָה
Groaning.	נְאָקָה

CHAP. 3.

Father-in-law.	חֹתֵן
Flame.	לַבָּה
Thorn-bush.	סְנֶה
Holiness. A holy thing.	קֹדֶשׁ
Task-master.	נֹגֵשׂ
Sorrow.	מַכְאֹב
Oppression.	לַחַץ
Memorial.	זֵכֶר
Wonders.	נִפְלָאוֹת
Favor.	חֵן

(46)

Neighbor (female).	שְׁכֶנֶת
Inhabitress.	גָּרָה

CHAP. 4.

Tail.	זָנָב
Snow.	שֶׁלֶג
Miracle.	מֹפֵת
A sharp instrument.	צֹר
Circumcision.	מוּלוֹת

CHAP. 5.

Pestilence.	דֶּבֶר
Magistrate.	שֹׁטֵר
Amount. Proportion.[1]	מַתְכֹּנֶת
Falsehood.	שֶׁקֶר
Stubble.	קַשׁ
Amount.	תֹּכֶן

CHAP. 6.

וארא

Judgments.	שְׁפָטִים
Heritage.	מוֹרָשָׁה
Shortness.	קֹצֶר
Aunt.	דּוֹדָה

CHAP. 7.

Sorcerer.	מְכַשֵּׁף
Secret arts.	לְהָטִים

---

[1] Ex. 30: 32.

Pond.	אֲגַם		
Secret arts.	לָטִים	Locusts.	אַרְבֶּה
Frog.	צְפַרְדֵעַ	Snare.	מוֹקֵשׁ
Kneading-trough.	מִשְׁאֶרֶת	Feast.	חַג
Respite.	רְוָחָה	Man.	גֶּבֶר
Lice.	כִּנָּם	Death.	מָוֶת
Finger.	אֶצְבַּע	Darkness.	אֲפֵלָה
Swarm.	עָרֹב	Hoof.	פַּרְסָה
Distinction.	פְּדֻת	Friend (fem).	רְעוּת
Two handfuls.	חָפְנַיִם	The middle (of night).	חֲצוֹת
Soot.	פִּיחַ	Mill-stones.	רֵחַיִם
Dust.	אָבָק	Dog.	כֶּלֶב
Inflammation.	שְׁחִין	Burning (of anger).	חֳרִי
Boils.	אֲבַעְבֻּעֹת	Neighbor.	שָׁכֵן
Plague.	מַגֵּפָה	Number. Amount.¹	מִכְסָה
Hail.	בָּרָד	Lamb.	כֶּבֶשׂ
Rain.	מָטָר	Door-post.	מְזוּזָה
Thunder.	קֹלֹת	Lintel.	מַשְׁקוֹף
Flax.	פִּשְׁתָּה	Bitter herbs.	מְרֹרִים
Barley.	שְׂעֹרָה	Legs.	כְּרָעַיִם
Green ears (of corn).	אָבִיב	Loins.	כְּתָנַיִם
Boll.	גִּבְעֹל	Haste.	חִפָּזוֹן
Wheat.	חִטָּה		
Spelt.	כֻּסֶּמֶת		

Left column chapter headings: CHAP. 8. (before Respite), CHAP. 9. (before Two handfuls).

Right column chapter headings: CHAP. 10. בא (before Locusts), CHAP. 11. (before Friend), CHAP. 12. (before Neighbor).

¹ Lev. 27 : 23.

Passover. Leaping.	פֶּסַח	The young (of cattle).	שֶׁגֶר
Plague.	נֶגֶף	Frontlets.	טוֹטָפֹת
Destruction. De-stroyer.	מַשְׁחִית	בשלח	
Memorial.	זִכָּרוֹן	Pillar.	עַמּוּד
Statute.	חֻקָּה	**CHAP. 14.**	
Leaven.	שְׂאוֹר	Warrior.	שָׁלִשׁ
That which is leavened.	חָמֵץ	Wall.	חוֹמָה
Convocation.	מִקְרָא	Watch.	אַשְׁמוּרָה
That which is leav-ened.	מַחְמֶצֶת	Wheel.	אֹפָן
Native.	אֶזְרָח	Heaviness.	כְּבֵדֻת
Bunch.	אֲגֻדָּה	**CHAP. 15.**	
Hyssop.	אֵזוֹב	Song.	שִׁירָה
Basin.	סַף	Strength.	עָז
The half.	חֲצִי	Depth.	מְצוֹלָה
Captive. Captivity.[1]	שְׁבִי	Excellence. Pride.[1]	גָּאוֹן
Dough.	בָּצֵק	Wrath.	חָרוֹן
Footmen.	רַגְלִי	Heap.	נֵד
Mixture. Woof.[2]	עֵרֶב	Floods.	נֹזְלִים
Observation.	שִׁמֻּרִים	Lead.	עוֹפֶרֶת
Hireling.	שָׂכִיר	Praise.	תְּהִלָּה
CHAP. 13.		Habitation.	נָוֶה
Firstling.	פֶּטֶר	Terror.	חִיל
Strength.	חֹזֶק	Mighty leaders.	אֵילִים
		Trembling.	רַעַד

---

[1] Deut. 21 : 13.   [2] Lev. 13 : 48.   [1] Lev. 26 : 19.

Greatness. A great act.[1]	גֹּדֶל
Place.	מָכוֹן
Dwelling. Sitting[2] (idly).	שֶׁבֶת
Sanctuary. A hallowed thing.[3]	מִקְדָּשׁ
Prophetess.	נְבִיאָה
Dance.	מָחוֹל
Disease.	מַחֲלָה
Palm-tree.	תָּמָר

CHAP. 16.

Pot.	סִיר
Satiety.	שֹׂבַע
A double portion. A copy.[4]	מִשְׁנֶה
Murmurings.	תְּלֻנֹּת
Quails.	שְׂלָו
Layer. Effusion.[5]	שְׁכָבָה
Something small. Dwarf.[6]	דַּק
Hoar-frost.	כְּפֹר
Omer (a measure). Sheaf.[7]	עֹמֶר
Head. Skull.	גֻּלְגֹּלֶת
Worms.	תּוֹלָעִים
Sabbath.	שַׁבָּתוֹן / שַׁבָּת

Worms.	רִמָּה
Manna.	מָן
Coriander.	גַּד
Taste.	טַעַם
Cake.	צַפִּיחִת
Vessel.	צִנְצֶנֶת
Ephah (a measure).	אֵיפָה

CHAP. 17.

Thirst.	צָמָא
Rock.	צוּר
Firmness. Faithfulness.[1]	אֱמוּנָה
Throne.	כֵּס

CHAP. 18.

יתרו

| Dismission. | שִׁלּוּחִים |
| Weariness. | תְּלָאָה |

CHAP. 19.

Eagle.	נֶשֶׁר
Treasure.	סְגֻלָּה
Thickness.	עָב
A jubilant sound. Jubilee.	יֹבֵל
Lightning. Glitter.[2]	בָּרָק
Cornet.	שֹׁפָר
The nether part.	תַּחְתִּית

[1] Deut. 10:21. [2] Ex. 21:10. [3] Num. 18:29. [4] Deut. 17:18. [5] Lev. 15:16. [6] Lev. 21:20. [7] Deut. 24:19.

[1] Deut. 32:4. [2] Deut. 32:41.

5

CHAP. 20.

A graven image.	פֶּסֶל
Similitude.	תְּמוּנָה
Descendants of the fourth generation.	רִבֵּעִים
Friend.	אֹהֵב
Falsehood.	שָׁוְא
Thick darkness.	עֲרָפֶל
Peace offering.	שְׁלָמִים
Hewn stone.	גָּזִית
Step.	מַעֲלָה

CHAP. 21.

מִשְׁפָּטִים

Person.	נֶפֶשׁ
Awl.	מַרְצֵעַ
Food. Kin.	שְׁאֵר
Marriage duty.	עֹנָה
Guile.	עָרְמָה
Fist.	אֶגְרֹף
Staff.	מִשְׁעֶנֶת
Judges.	פְּלִלִים
Burning.	כְּוִיָּה
Ransom.	פִּדְיוֹן

CHAP. 22.

| Burglary. | מַחְתֶּרֶת |
| Thief. | גַּנָּב |

The guilt of murder.	דָּמִים
Theft.	גְּנֵבָה
Stack.	גָּדִישׁ
Standing corn.	קָמָה
Burning.	בְּעֵרָה
Garment.	שַׂלְמָה
A lost thing.	אֲבֵדָה
Witch.	מְכַשֵּׁפָה
A fatherless child.	יָתוֹם
Claimant.	נֹשֶׁה
Usury.	נֶשֶׁךְ
Abundance.	מְלֵאָה
Tear. The juice of grapes and olives.	דֶּמַע
Burden.	מַשָּׂא
Bribe.	שֹׁחַד
The clear sighted.	פִּקֵּחַ
Times.	רְגָלִים
First fruits.	בִּכּוּרִים
Harvest.	אָסִיף
Male.	זָכוּר
Adversary.	צָרֵר
Hornet.	צִרְעָה
Wilderness.	שְׁמָמָה

CHAP. 24.

Basin.	אַגָּן
Brick-work.	לְבֵנָה
Sapphire.	סַפִּיר
Purity. Purification.[1]	טֹהַר
A noble.	אָצִיל
Tablet.	לוּחַ
Attendant.	מְשָׁרֵת

CHAP. 25.

תרומה

Offering.	תְּרוּמָה
Bluish thread.	תְּכֵלֶת
Purple thread.	אַרְגָּמָן
Scarlet thread. Worms.[2]	תּוֹלַעַת
Goat's hair.	עִזִּים
Badger.	תַּחַשׁ
Acacias.	שִׁטִּים
Spice.	בֶּשֶׂם
Anointing. A hallowed portion.[3]	מִשְׁחָה
Incense.	קְטֹרֶת
Spices.	סַמִּים
Setting (of gems).	מִלּוּאָה
Ephod.	אֵפוֹד

Breast plate.	חֹשֶׁן
Pattern.	תַּבְנִית
Tabernacle.	מִשְׁכָּן
Festoon.	זֵר
Bars.	בַּדִּים
Testimony.	עֵדֻת
Cover.	כַּפֹּרֶת
Chase work.	מִקְשָׁה
Table.	שֻׁלְחָן
Border.	מִסְגֶּרֶת
Hand-breadth.	טֹפַח
Corner. Side.[1]	פֵּאָה
Dish.	קְעָרָה
Supporters.	קְשׂוֹת
Purifiers.	מְנַקִּיֹּת
Show bread.	לֶחֶם פָּנִים
Candlestick.	מְנוֹרָה
Knob.	כַּפְתֹּר
Bud. Flower.	פֶּרַח
Lamp.	נֵר
Tongs.	מֶלְקָחַיִם
Snuff dish. Censer.[1]	מַחְתָּה

---

[1] Lev. 12 : 4. [2] Deut. 28 :39. [3] Lev. 7 : 35.

[1] Ex. 26: 18. [2] Ex. 27: 3.

CHAP. 26.		Fork.	מַזְלֵג
Curtain.	יְרִיעָה	Grate.	מִכְבָּר
Artist.	חֹשֵׁב	Net.	רֶשֶׁת
Measure.	מִדָּה	Cornice.	כַּרְכֹּב
Loops.	לֻלָאֹת	Hangings.	קְלָעִים
Junction.	{ חֹבֶרֶת / מַחְבֶּרֶת }	Fillets.	חֲשֻׁקִים
		The east.	מִזְרָח
Hooks.	קְרָסִים	Side. Shoulder.[1]	כָּתֵף
Flap.	סֶרַח	Pin. Spaddle.[2]	יָתֵד
Rear.	אָחֹור	**CHAP. 28.**	
Board.	קֶרֶשׁ		תצוה
Tenons.	יָדֹות	Ornament.	תִּפְאָרֶת
South.	תֵּימָן	Wisdom.	חָכְמָה
Base.	אֶדֶן	Robe.	מְעִיל
Corner.	מִקְצֹוּעַ	Mitre.	מִצְנֶפֶת
Bolt.	בְּרִיחַ	Girdle.	אַבְנֵט
Receptacles.	בָּתִּים	Shoulder-pieces.	כְּתֵפֹת
Vail.	פָּרֹכֶת	Belt.	חֵשֶׁב
Hooks.	וָוִים	Girding.	אֲפֻדָּה
Curtain.	מָסָךְ	Engraver.	חָרָשׁ
Embroiderer.	רֹקֵם	Engraving.	פִּתוּחַ
CHAP. 27.		Sockets.	מִשְׁבְּצֹת
Corner.	פִּנָּה	Chains.	שַׁרְשְׁרֹת
Shovels.	יָעִים	Knots (at the ends of strings).	מִגְבָּלֹת
Sprinkling-basin.	מִזְרָק		

---

[1] Num. 7: 9.　　[2] Deut. 23: 14.

Wreathen work.	עֲבֹת	Frontal. Blossom.[1]	צִיץ
Span.	זֶרֶת	Forehead.	מֵצַח
Row.	טוּר	Cap.	מִגְבָּעָה
Sardius.	אֹדֶם	Breeches.	מִכְנָסַיִם
Topaz.	פִּטְדָה	Linen. Portion.[2]	בַּד

CHAP. 29.

Emerald.	בָּרֶקֶת	Cake.	חַלָּה
Carbuncle.	נֹפֶךְ	Wafer.	רָקִיק
Diamond.	יַהֲלֹם	Diadem. Abstinence.[3]	נֵזֶר
Opal.	לֶשֶׁם	Priesthood.	כְּהֻנָּה
Turquoise.	שְׁבוֹ	Base.	יְסוֹד
Amethyst.	אַחְלָמָה	Caul.	יֹתֶרֶת
Chrysolite.	תַּרְשִׁישׁ	Liver.	כָּבֵד
Jasper.	יָשְׁפֶה	Kidneys.	כְּלָיוֹת
Chains.	שַׁרְשֹׁת	Dung.	פֶּרֶשׁ
Knot-work.	גַּבְלֻת	Piece.	נֵתַח
Urim.	אוּרִים	Sacrifice.	אִשֶּׁה
Tummim.	תֻּמִּים	Tip (of the ear).	תְּנוּךְ
The whole.	כָּלִיל	Thumb. The big toe.	בֹּהֶן
Weaver.	אֹרֵג	Tail.	אַלְיָה
Habergeon.	תַּחְרָא	Shoulder.	שׁוֹק
The lower hem.	שׁוּלִים	Consecration.	מִלֻּאִים
Pomegranate.	רִמּוֹן	Waving. Heaving.	תְּנוּפָה
Bell.	פַּעֲמֹן		

[1] Num. 17: 23.   [2] Ex. 30: 34.   [3] Num. 6: 4.

5*

Breast (of cattle).	חָזֶה	Onycha.	שְׁחֵלֶת
Portion.	מָנָה	Galbanum.	חֶלְבְּנָה
Stranger.	זָר	Frankincense.	לְבֹנָה
Atonement.	כִּפֻּרִים	**CHAP. 31.**	
A tenth part.	עִשָּׂרֹן	Understanding.	תְּבוּנָה
		Knowledge.	דַּעַת
A fourth part.	רֶבַע רְבִיעִת	Artistic work.	חֲרֹשֶׁת
		Knitted cloth.	שָׂרָד
Hin (a measure).	הִין	**CHAP. 32.**	
CHAP. 30.		A graving tool.	חֶרֶט
Incension.	מִקְטָר	Calf. Heifer.	עֵגֶל
Roof.	גַּג	Casting.	מַסֵּכָה
Well.	קִיר	Writing.	מִכְתָּב
כי תשא		Shouting.	רֵעַ
The half.	מַחֲצִית	Victory. Mighty deeds.[1]	גְּבוּרָה
Gerah (a weight). Cud.[1]	גֵּרָה	Defeat.	חֲלוּשָׁה
Laver.	כִּיּוֹר	Shame.	שִׁמְצָה
Myrrh.	מוֹר	**CHAP. 33.**	
Cinnamon.	קִנָּמוֹן	Ornament.	עֲדִי
Spice.	בֹּשֶׂם	Moment.	רֶגַע
Cassia.	קִדָּה	Son.	בֵּן
Composition.	רֹקַח	Cleft.	נִקְרָה
Compounding.	מִרְקַחַת	**CHAP. 34.**	
Compounder.	רֹקֵחַ	A hallowed grove.	אֲשֵׁרָה
Stacte.	נָטָף	Revolution (of the year or season.)	תְּקוּפָה

Vail.	מָסְוֶה	Mirrors.	מַרְאוֹת
CHAP. 35.		Overlaying.	צִפּוּי
ויקהל		CHAP. 39.	
Cords.	מֵיתָרִים	פְקוּדֵי	
Clasp.	חָח	Plates.	פַּחִים
Bead.	כּוּמָז	Ornament.	פְּאֵר
Spun thread.	מַטְוֶה	Row.	מַעֲרָכָה
Free-will offering.	נְדָבָה	Array. Valuation.[1]	עֵרֶךְ
CHAP. 38.		Anointing. A hallowed portion.[2]	כְּמִשְׁחָה
Ends.	קְצוֹת		

LEVITICUS.

Offering.	ויקרא קָרְבָּן	Full ears.	כַּרְמֶל
Fat.	פֶּדֶר	CHAP. 3.	
Crop.	מֻרְאָה	Flanks.	כְּסָלִים
Excrement.	נֹצָה	Back-bone.	עָצֶה
Ashes.	דֶּשֶׁן	CHAP. 4.	
CHAP. 2.		Error.	שְׁגָגָה
Memorial.	אַזְכָּרָה	Guilt.	אַשְׁמָה
Baking.	מַאֲפֶה	A place where ashes are thrown.	שֶׁפֶךְ
A shallow pan.	מַחֲבַת	She-goat.	שְׂעִירָה
A deep pan.	מַרְחֶשֶׁת	CHAP. 5.	
Crushed grain.	גֶּרֶשׂ	Carcass.	נְבֵלָה

[1] Lev. 6: 15.　　[2] Num. 18: 8.

Defilement.	טֻמְאָה	Fins.	סְנַפִּיר
Ewe-lamb.	כִּשְׂבָּה	Scales.	קַשְׂקֶשֶׂת
A tenth part.	עֲשִׂירִת	Ossifrage.	פֶּרֶס
Perfidy.	מַעַל	Ospray.	עָזְנִיָּה
Fellow-being.	עָמִית	Vulture.	דָּאָה
Deposit.	תְּשׂוּמֶת יָד	Kite.	אַיָּה
		Ostrich.	בַּת הַיַּעֲנָה
Goods taken forcibly.	{ גָּזֵל / גְּזֵלָה	Night-hawk.	תַּחְמָס
Goods obtained by fraud.	עֹשֶׁק	Cuckoo.	שַׁחַף
CHAP. 6.		Cormorant.	שָׁלָךְ
צַו		Great owl.	יַנְשׁוּף
Fire-place.	מוֹקְדָה	Snail. Mole.	תִּנְשֶׁמֶת
Garment.	מַד	Pelican.	קָאַת
Cakes twice baked.	תְּפִינִים	Gier-eagle.	רָחָם
Earthen-ware.	חֶרֶשׂ	Stork.	חֲסִידָה
CHAP. 7.		Heron.	אֲנָפָה
Thanksgiving.	תּוֹדָה	Lapwing.	דוּכִיפַת
Abomination.	שֶׁקֶץ	Bat.	עֲטַלֵּף
CHAP. 10.		Bald locust.	סָלְעָם
שְׁמִינִי		Beetle.	חַרְגֹּל
Uncle.	דֹּד	Grasshopper.	חָגָב
Intoxicating drink.	שֵׁכָר	Weasel.	חֹלֶד
CHAP. 11.		Mouse.	עַכְבָּר
Slit.	שֶׁסַע	Tortoise.	צָב
Cony.	שָׁפָן		
Hare.	אַרְנֶבֶת		
Swine.	חֲזִיר		

Ferret. אֲנָקָה

Lizard. לְטָאָה

Snail. חֹמֶט

Furnace. כִּירַיִם

Vegetable. זֵרוּעַ

CHAP. 12.
תזריע

Separation. נִדָּה

Indisposition (from the menses). דָּוֺת

Purification. טָהֳרָה

Source. מָקוֹר

A woman in child-bed. יֹלֶדֶת

CHAP. 13.

Swelling. סַפַּחַת

Spot. בַּהֶרֶת

Leprosy. צָרַעַת

Swelling. מִסְפַּחַת

Scab. צָרֶבֶת

Burn. מִכְוָה

A bearded chin. זָקָן

Scall. נֶתֶק

Freckle. בֹּהַק

Baldness. A bare spot on the inside of a garment. קָרַחַת

Baldness on the front part of the head. A bare spot on the outside of a garment. גַּבַּחַת

Leper. צָרוּעַ

Mustache. שָׂפָם

Wool. צֶמֶר

Flag. פִּשְׁתִּים

Warp. • שְׁתִי

Corrosion. פְּחֶתֶת

CHAP. 14.
מצרע

Leper. מְצֹרָע

Cedar. אֶרֶז

Brows (of the eyes). גַּבּוֹת

Log (a measure). לֹג

CHAP. 15. •

Fluxion. זוֹב

Something to ride in, or upon. מֶרְכָּב

CHAP. 16.
אחרי מות

Lot. גּוֹרָל

Azazel.¹ עֲזָאזֵל

A live coal. גַּחֶלֶת

CHAP. 18.

Kinswoman. שְׁאֵרָה

---

[1] Many conjectures have been made as to the meaning of this word. I am inclined to believe it is the proper name of the particular place where the goat was to be sent.

A seminal effusion.	שִׁכְבַת	Measure (of liquids).	מְשׂוּרָה
Wicked thought.	זִמָּה	Balance.	מֹאזְנַיִם
Confusion.	תֶּבֶל		

CHAP. 19.

קדושים

| Idols. | אֱלִילִם | | |

CHAP. 20.

| | | Adulterer. | נֹאֵף |
| Gleaning. | לֶקֶט | Adulteress. | נֹאֶפֶת |

CHAP. 21.

אמור

Scattered grapes.	פֶּרֶט	Baldness.	קָרְחָה
Wages.	פְּעֻלָה	Incision.	שָׂרֶטֶת
Stumbling-block.	מִכְשׁוֹל	A profane woman.	חֲלָלָה
Injustice.	עָוֶל	Virginity.	בְּתוּלִים
Righteousness.	צֶדֶק	Blemish.	מוּם
Tale-bearer.	רָכִיל	A streak running from the white of the eye into the pupil.	תְּבַלֻל
Admixture (of species, of seed, or of wool and linen).	כִּלְאַיִם	Scurf.	גָרָב
A texture of wool and linen.	שַׁעַטְנֵז	Itch.	יַלֶּפֶת
Freedom.	חֻפְשָׁה	Testicles.	אֶשֶׁךְ
A woman under sentence of being lashed.	בִּקֹרֶת	Blindness.	עַוֶּרֶת
Praises.	הִלּוּלִים	Wen.	יַבֶּלֶת
Incision.	שֶׂרֶט	Corruption.	מָשְׁחָת
Marking.	כְּתֹבֶת	Parched corn.	קָלִי
Pricking on the flesh.	קַעֲקַע	Assembling. Restraining.	עֲצֶרֶת
Exorcism.	אוֹב	Branch.	עָנָף
Divination.	יִדְּעֹנִי	Willows.	עֲרָבִים

Row.	מַעֲרֶכֶת	Bar.	מוֹטָה

CHAP. 25. **בהר**		Erectness.	קוֹמְמִיּוּת
That which grows spontaneously.	סָפִיחַ	Terror.	בֶּהָלָה
		Consumption.	שַׁחֶפֶת
Sounding (of a trumpet).	תְּרוּעָה	Burning fever.	קַדַּחַת
Freedom.	דְּרוֹר	Vanity.	רִיק
Sale.	מִמְכָּר	Copper.	נְחֻשָׁה
Conclusiveness.	צְמִתֻת	Contrariety.	קֶרִי
Redemption. Ransom.	גְּאֻלָּה	Plague.	מַכָּה
Kinsman. Avenger.[1]	גֹּאֵל	Vengeance.	נָקָם
Suburbs.	מִגְרָשׁ	A high place.	בָּמָה
Increase.	{ תַּרְבִּית / מַרְבִּית }	Sun-images.	חַמָּנִים
		Idols.	גִּלּוּלִים
Sale.	מִמְכֶּרֶת	Waste.	חָרְבָּה
Descendant.	עֵקֶר	Panic.	מֹרֶךְ
Purchaser.	קֹנֶה	Flight.	מְנוּסָה
CHAP. 26. Hieroglyphic.	מַשְׂכִּית	Pursuer.	רֹדֵף
בחקתי		Power to stand.	תְּקוּמָה
Produce.	יְבוּל	**CHAP. 27.** Exchange.	תְּמוּרָה
Threshing.	דַּיִשׁ	Barley.	שְׂעֹרִים
Vintage.	בָּצִיר	A doomed thing.	חֵרֶם

[1] Num. 35: 19.

NUMBERS.

במדבר

Standard.	דֶּגֶל
Anger.	קֶצֶף

CHAP. 3.

Superintendence. Visitation.[1]	פְּקֻדָּה
Covering.	כָּסוּי
Supporters.	קָשׂוֹת
Bar.	מוֹט

CHAP. 5.

נשא

Jealousy. Indignation.[2]	קִנְאָה
Floor.	קַרְקַע

CHAP. 6.

Vinegar.	חֹמֶץ
Infusion.	מִשְׁרָה
Kernels.	חַרְצַנִּים
Husk.	זָג
Razor.	תַּעַר
Disorderliness.	פֶּרַע
Suddenness.	פֶּתַע
Dedication.	חֲנֻכָּה

CHAP. 8.

בהעלתך

Firstling.	פִּטְרָה

CHAP. 10.

Trumpet.	חֲצוֹצְרָה
Rearward.	מְאַסֵּף
Enemy.	מְשַׂנֵּא

CHAP. 11.

Rabble.	אַסְפְסֻף
Cucumbers.	קִשֻּׁאִים
Melons.	אֲבַטִּחִים
Leek.	חָצִיר
Onions.	בְּצָלִים
Garlic.	שׁוּמִים
Mortar.	מְדֹכָה
Pot.	פָּרוּר
A fresh cake.	לָשָׁד
Nurser.	אֹמֵן
Suckling.	יֹנֵק
Aversion.	זָרָא
A young man.	בָּחוּר
Allegory.	חִידָה

שלח לך

Open cities.	מַחֲנִים
A fortified city.	מִבְצָר
Giant.	עֲנָק

[1] Num. 16: 29.   [2] Num. 25: 11.

Branch.	זְמוֹרָה	Pole. Sign.[1]	נֵס

CHAP. 14.

Prey.	בַּז	Ruins.	עִיִּים
Greatness.	גָּדֵל	Discharge.	אֲשֶׁד
Backsliding.	זְנוּת	A noble.	נָדִיב
Alienation.	תְּנוּאָה	Desert.	יְשִׁימֹן

CHAP. 15.

A third part.	שְׁלִשִׁית	Flame.	לֶהָבָה
Dough.	עֲרִיסָה	Captivity.	שְׁבִית
Fringes.	צִיצִית	One who escaped.	שָׂרִיד

CHAP. 16. קרח

CHAP. 22

Creation.	בְּרִיאָה	Plain.	עֲרָבָה

בלק

CHAP. 17.

Plating.	רִקֻּעַ	Environs.	סְבִיבֹת
Rebellion.	מְרִי	Divination. Things employed in divination.	קֶסֶם

CHAP. 18.

Oil.	יִצְהָר	Adversary.	שָׂטָן
Exchange.	חֵלֶף	A narrow path	מִשְׁעוֹל
Winepress.	יֶקֶב	Fence.	גָּדֵר

CHAP. 20. חקת

CHAP. 23.

Rock.	סֶלַע	Hill.	שְׁפִי
Highway.	מְסִלָּה	Parable. Proverb.[2]	מָשָׁל
Price.	מֶכֶר	Mountain.	הֲרַר

CHAP. 21.

Spices.	אֲתָרִים	A fourth part.	רֹבַע
Serpent.	שָׂרָף	Watchman.	צֹפֶה
		Son (poetically).	בְּנוֹ

---

[1] Num. 26: 10.   [2] Deut. 28: 37.

Iniquity. Mourning.[1]	אָוֶן	**CHAP. 31**	
Strength.	תּוֹעָפֹת	Vengeance.	נְקָמָה
Buffalo.	רְאֵם	Prey.	מַלְקוֹחַ
Enchantment.	נַחַשׁ	Tin.	בְּדִיל
Lion.	אֲרִי	Tribute.	מֶכֶס
CHAP. 24.		The half.	מֶחֱצָה
Lign aloes.	אֲהָלִים	Chain.	אֶצְעָדָה
Bucket.	דְּלִי	Ear-ring.	עָגִיל
Kingdom.	מַלְכוּת	**CHAP. 32.**	
Possession.	יְרֵשָׁה	Brood.	תַּרְבּוּת
Destruction.	אֹבֵד	A fenced place.	גְּדֵרָה
Extermination.	בָּעֵר	Village.	חַוָּה
Ship.	צִי	Adjacent places.	בָּנוֹת
CHAP. 25.		**CHAP. 33.** מסעי	
Javelin.	רֹמַח		
Tent.	קֻבָּה	Thorns.	שִׂכִּים
Stomach.	קֵבָה	Prickles.	צְנִינִם
פנחם		**CHAP. 34.**	
Wiles.	נְכָלִים	Ascent.	מַעֲלֵה
CHAP. 27.		Confines.	תּוֹצָאֹת
Dignity.	הוֹד		
CHAP. 30. מטות		**CHAP. 35.**	
Bond.	אִסָּר	Refuge.	מִקְלָט
Utterance.	מִבְטָא	Manslayer.	רֹצֵחַ
Expression. A going out.[2]	מוֹצָא	Hatred.	שִׂנְאָה
		Premeditation.	צְדִיָּה

[1] Deut. 26: 14.   [2] Num. 33: 2.

DEUTERONOMY.

דברים

Low land.	שְׁפֵלָה
Cumbrance.	טֹרַח
Bee.	דְּבֹרָה

CHAP. 2.
A foot-breadth.	מִדְרָךְ
Possession.	יְרֵשָׁה
City.	קִרְיָה

CHAP. 3.
Tract of land.	חֶבֶל
Level country.	מִישֹׁר
Bedstead.	עֶרֶשׂ
Ravines.	אֶשְׁדֹּת

ואתחנן

| Valley. | גַּיְא |

CHAP. 4.
Understanding.	בִּינָה
Figure.	סֶמֶל
Furnace.	כּוּר
Trial.	מַסָּה

CHAP. 6.
| Might. | מְאֹד |

CHAP. 7.

עקב

| Cattle. | אֲלָפִים |

Increase (of the flock).	עַשְׁתְּרוֹת
Sickness.	חֳלִי
Disease.	מַדְוֶה
Disturbance.	מְהוּמָה

CHAP. 8.
Scarcity.	מִסְכֵּנֻת
Scorpion.	עַקְרָב
Drought.	צִמָּאוֹן
Flint.	חַלָּמִישׁ
Strength.	עֹצֶם

CHAP. 9.
Wickedness.	רִשְׁעָה
Uprightness.	יֹשֶׁר
Stubbornness.	קְשִׁי
Wickedness.	רֶשַׁע

CHAP. 10.
| Fearful acts. | נוֹרָאֹת |

CHAP. 11.
Chastisement.	מוּסָר
Greens.	יָרָק
The first rain.	יוֹרֶה
The latter rain.	מַלְקוֹשׁ

ראה

| Setting (of the sun). | מָבוֹא |

(63)

CHAP. 12.

Dwelling.	שָׁכֵן
Occupation.	מִשְׁלַח יָד
Desire.	אַוָּה
Roe buck.	צְבִי
Hart.	אַיָּל

CHAP. 13.

Departing (from duty).	סָרָה
Secret.	סֵתֶר
A heap of ruins.	תֵּל

CHAP. 14.

Fallow deer.	יַחְמוּר
The wild goat.	אַקּוֹ
Gazelle.	דִּישֹׁן
The wild ox.	תְּאוֹ
Antelope.	זֶמֶר
Glede.	רָאָה
Vulture.	דַּיָּה
Gier-eagle.	רָחָמָה

CHAP. 15.

Release.	שְׁמִטָּה
Debt.	מַשֶּׁה
Need.	מַחְסֹר

OHAP. 16.

| Sickle. | חֶרְמֵשׁ |
| Proportion. | מִסָּה |

CHAP. 17.

שפטים

| Plea. | דִּין |
| Presumption. | זָדוֹן |

CHAP. 18.

Cheeks.	לְחָיַיִם
Maw.	קֵבָה
Fleece.	גֵּז
Observer of times.	מְעוֹנֵן
Enchanter.	מְנַחֵשׁ

CHAP. 19.

| Forest. | יַעַר |
| Ax. | גַּרְזֶן |

CHAP. 20.

| Siege. Bulwark. | מָצוֹר |

CHAP. 21.

כי תצא

Captivity. Captives.	שִׁבְיָה
Nail.	צִפֹּרֶן
Glutton.	זוֹלֵל
Drunkard.	סֹבֵא

CHAP. 22.

Young birds.	אֶפְרֹחִים
Eggs.	בֵּיצִים
Battlement.	מַעֲקֶה
Fringes.	גְּדִילִים
Actions.	עֲלִילֹת

CHAP. 23.	
Crushing.	דִּכָּה
Privy member.	שָׁפְכָה
One of spurious descent.	מַמְזֵר
Accident.	מִקְרֶה
Utensil.	אָזֵן
Excrement.	צֵאָה
Sodomite.	קָדֵשׁ
Prostitution hire.	אֶתְנַן
Price.	מְחִיר
Ears of corn.	מְלִילֹת
CHAP. 24.	
Divorcement.	כְּרִיתֻת
Debt.	מַשָּׁאָה
Pledge.	עֲבֹט
CHAP. 25.	
A husband's brother.	יָבָם
A brother's wife.	יְבֶמֶת
Pudenda.	מְבֻשִׁים
Bag.	כִּים
CHAP. 26.	
	כי תבא
Basket.	טֶנֶא
Defilement.	טָמֵא
Dwelling.	מָעוֹן

CHAP. 27.	
Plaster.	שִׂיד
Mother-in-law.	חֹתֶנֶת
CHAP. 28.	
Storehouse.	אָסָם
Treasure.	אוֹצָר
Curse.	מְאֵרָה
Rebuke.	מִגְעֶרֶת
Acts.	מַעֲלָלִים
Inflammation.	דַּלֶּקֶת
Intense heat.	חַרְחֻר
Blasting.	שִׁדָּפוֹן
Mildew.	יֵרָקוֹן
Horror.	זַעֲוָה
Hemorrhoids.	עֲפָלִים / טְחוֹרִים
Itch.	חֶרֶם
Madness.	שִׁגָּעוֹן
Blindness.	עִוָּרוֹן
Confusion.	תִּמָּהוֹן
Astonishment.	שַׁמָּה
Satire.	שְׁנִינָה
Cricket.	צְלָצַל
Nakedness.	עֵירֹם
Want.	חֹסֶר

C*

Straightness.	מָצוֹק	Howling.	יְלֵל
Tenderness.	רֹך	Pupil (of the eye).	אִישׁוֹן
After-birth.	שִׁלְיָה	Pinion.	אֶבְרָה
Failing.	כִּלָּיוֹן	Produce.	תְּנוּבָה
Languor.	דִּאָבוֹן	Field (poet).	שָׂדַי

CHAP. 29.

נצבים

		Wine (poet).	חֶמֶר
Abomination.	שִׁקּוּץ	God.	אֱלוֹהַ
Root.	שֹׁרֶשׁ	Demons.	שֵׁדִים
Wormwood.	לַעֲנָה	Provocation.	כַּעַס
Stubbornness.	שְׁרִרוּת	Perverseness.	תַּהְפֻּכֹת
Satiety.	רָוָה	Faith.	אֵמֻן
Thirst.	צִמְאָה	Vanity.	הֶבֶל
Diseases.	תַּחֲלוּאִים	Foundations.	מוֹסָדוֹת
Overthrow.	מַהְפֵּכָה	Burning heat.	רֶשֶׁף
Hidden things.	נִסְתָּרוֹת	Destruction.	קֶטֶב

CHAP. 30.

		Wild beasts.	בְּהֵמֹת
Captivity.	שְׁבוּת	Counsel.	עֵצָה
Expulsion.	נִדָּח	Fields.	שְׁרֵמֹת
		Poison.	רוֹשׁ

CHAP. 32.

האזינו

		Asp.	פֶּתֶן
Doctrine.	לֶקַח	Recompense.	שִׁלֵּם
Heavy rains.	רְבִיבִים	Calamity.	אֵיד
Work.	פֹּעַל	Things to come.	עֲתִדֹת
Waste.	תֹּהוּ	Protection.	סִתְרָה

CHAP. 33.

הברכה

Law.	דָּת	Abundance.	שֶׁפַע
Word.	דִּבְּרָה	The south.	דָּרוֹם
Congregation.	קְהִלָּה	Bolt.	מִנְעָל
Incense.	קְטוֹרָה	Old age.	דִּבֵא
A beloved one.	יְדִיד	Excellency.	גַּאֲוָה
A precious thing.	מֶגֶד	Heaven.	שְׁחָקִים
Produce.	גֶּרֶשׂ	Habitation.	מְעֹנָה
Extremity.	אֶפֶס		

CHAP. 34.

Valley.	גַּי
Freshness.	לֵחַ

VERBS.

The figures attached to the roots indicate that the verb appears in the 2d, 3d, 4th, 5th, 6th, or 7th form of conjugation.

Verbs in which one of the radicals is omitted, or to which any serviles are added, have the radix attached to them, and should be looked for in the index, under the letter with which the *root* begins.

Verbs in the infinitive have the accent invariably on the last syllable, except those ending in חַ, עַ and הַ ; and those having the vowels — — or ֻ — ֻ, which have the accent on the penultimate.

GENESIS.

בראשית

To create.	בָּרָא
To be.	הָיָה· הֱיוֹת
To hover.	רָחַף
To say. Avouch.[1]	אָמַר
To See. Provide.[2]	רָאָה· רְאוֹת
To Separate. Distinguish.[3] [5 בדל]	הַבְדִּיל·
To call. Read. Meet.	קָרָא
To make. Do. Work.[1] Acquire[2]. Prepare.[3]	עָשָׂה
To be gathered. [2 קוה]	הִקָּוֶה
To appear. Be seen.[4] [2 ראה]	הֵרָאָה
To produce herbage.· [5 רשא]	הַדְשָׁא
To bear seed. Be pregnant.[5] [5 זרע]	הַזְרִיעַ
To bring out. Bring forth. [5 יצא]	הוֹצִיא

---

[1] Deut. 6: 17.   [2] Gen. 22: 8.   [3] Lev. 10: 10.

[1] Ex. 31: 4.   [2] Gen. 12: 5.   [3] Gen. 18: 7.   [4] Ex. 13: 7.   [5] Lev. 12: 2.

To be light. Lighten.	אוֹר
To give. Place. Render.	נָתֹן. תֵּת
To rule.	מָשַׁל
To creep. Abound.	שָׁרַץ
To fly.	עוּף
To creep.	רָמַשׂ
To bless. [3]	בָּרַךְ
To bear fruit.	פָּרָה
To increase. Be great, or numerous.	רָבָה
To fill. Be full. Persevere.[1]	מָלֵא
To rule.	רָדָה
To subdue.	כָּבַשׁ
To bear seed. Sow.[2]	זָרַע

CHAP. 2.

To be finished. To be at an end.[3]	כָּלָה
To finish. Consume.[4] [3]	כָּלָה
To rest. Cease.[5]	שָׁבַת
To be holy. Set apart.	קָדַשׁ
To sprout.	צָמַח
To cause to rain. [5 מטר]	הַמְטִיר
To labor. Serve.	עָבַד

[1] Num. 32:11. [2] Gen. 26:12. [3] Gen. 21:15. [4] Gen. 41:30. [5] Gen. 8:22.

To go up.	עָלָה. עֲלוֹת
To water. Give to drink. [5 שקה]	הַשְׁקָה
To form. Be distressed.[1]	יָצַר
To blow.	נָפַח
To plant.	נָטַע
To place. Set. Render.[2]	שׂוֹם
To go out. Come forth.	יָצָא. צֵאת
To desire.	חָמַד
To separate. Scatter.[3] [2 פרד]	הַפָּרֵד
To surround. Turn.[4] Be changed.[5]	סָבַב
To go.	הָלַךְ. לֶכֶת
To take. Undertake.[6]	לָקַח. קַחַת
To place. Leave.[7] [5 ינח]	הַנִּיחַ
To keep. Guard. Observe.	שָׁמַר
To command. [3]	צִוָּה
To eat. Consume.	אָכַל
To die.	מוּת
To bring. [5 בוא]	הֵבִיא
To find. Befall.[8] Suffice.[9]	מָצָא

[1] Gen. 32:8. [2] Ex. 4:11. [3] Gen. 10:5. [4] Gen. 42:24. [5] Num. 32:38; 36:7. [6] Num. 16:1; 23; 20. [7] Gen. 42:33. [8] Gen. 44:34. [9] Num. 11:22.

To fall.	נָפַל	To beget.	יָלַד. לֶדֶת
To sleep.	יָשֵׁן	To return.	שׁוּב
To close.	סָגַר	To clothe.	לָבַשׁ
To build.	בָּנָה	To send. Extend.	שָׁלַח
To leave. Withdraw.[1] Loosen;[2]	עֹזֵב	To live. Revive.[1]	חָיָה.
To cleave.	דָּבַק	To drive. Expel.	גָּרַשׁ
To be ashamed.	בּוֹשׁ	To dwell. Rest.[2]	שָׁכַן
		To turn. Overturn.	הָפַךְ

CHAP. 3.

CHAP. 4.

To touch. Strike.[3]	נָגַע	To be pregnant.	הָרָה
To know. Distinguish.[4]	יָדַע דַּעַת	To acquire. Buy.	קָנָה
To open (the eyes).	פָּקַח	To continue. Do again. Add.	יָסַף
To make wise. Act wisely. [5 שכל] Understand.[5]	הַשְׂכִּיל	To have regard.	שָׁעָה
To twist.	תָּפֹר	To burn (with anger).	חָרָה
To hear. Understand.	שָׁמַע	To do good. Put in order.[3] [5 יטב]	הֵיטִיב
To hide oneself. [2 חבא]	הֵחָבֵא	To lie down. Rest upon.[4]	רָבַץ
To fear.	יָרֵא	To arise. Stand.	קוּם
To tell. [5 נגד]	הִגִּיד	To kill.	הָרַג
To beguile. [5 נשא]	הִשִּׁיא	To cry out.	צָעַק
To curse.	אָרַר	To open widely.	פָּצָה
To put. Place.	שׁוּת	To move.	נוּעַ
To bruise.	שׁוּף	To wander.	נוּד

---

¹ Gen. 24: 27. ² Ex. 23: 5. ³ Gen. 12: 17; 32: 25. ⁴ Gen. 18: 19. ⁵ Deut. 32: 29. ⁶ Ex. 33: 12.

¹ Gen. 45: 27. ² Num. 9: 17; Deut. 33: 20. ³ Ex. 30: 7. ⁴ Deut. 29: 19.

To bear. Lift up. Respect.[1] Pardon.[2] Pronounce.[3]	נָשָׂא · שָׂאֵת
To be hidden. [סתר 2]	הִסָּתֵר
To avenge.	נָקֹם
To smite. Strike. [נכה 5]	הַכֵּה. הַכּוֹת
To dwell. Sit. Abide.	יָשֹׁב. שֶׁבֶת
To be born. [ילד 2]	הִוָּלֵד
To take hold. Handle. [תפש]	הָפֹשׂ
To forge.	לָטֹשׁ
To listen. [אזן 5]	הַאֲזִין
To begin. Profane.[4] [חלל 5]	הָחֵל

CHAP. 5.

To comfort. [3]	נָחֵם

CHAP. 6.

To increase. Shoot.[5]	רָבָב
To choose.	בָּחֹר
To pronounce, or execute judgment.	דּוֹן. דִּין
To repent. Be comforted. [נחם 2]	הִנָּחֵם
To grieve.	עָצֵב
To blot out. Reach.[6]	מָחֹה

נח

To destroy. Corrupt. [3]	שָׁחֵת
To come. Go.[1] Set (of the sun).	בּוֹא
To daub.	כָּפֹר
To perish.	גָּוַע
To raise. Establish. [קום 5]	הָקִים
To gather. Withdraw.[2]	אָסֹף

CHAP. 7.

To cleave asunder.	בָּקַע
To open.	פָּתֹחַ
To rise. Arise, or grow out.[3]	רוֹם
To prevail.	גָּבֹר
To cover. Conceal.	כָּסֹה
To be left. [שאר 2]	הִשָּׁאֵר

CHAP. 8.

To remember.	זָכֹר
To pass.	עָבֹר
To abate.	שָׁכֹךְ
To be shut up. [סכר 2]	הִסָּכֵר
To restrain	כָּלֹא
To be wanting. Lack.	חָסֹר
To rest.	נוֹחַ

[1] Gen. 19: 21. [2] Gen. 18: 24. [3] Ex. 20: 7; Num. 23: 7. [4] Num. 30: 2. [5] Gen. 49: 23. [6] Num. 34: 11.

[1] Gen. 16: 2; 37: 30. [2] Gen. 49 33. [3] Ex. 18: 20

To be dried up. Be dry.	יָבֵשׁ
To be light. Diminished.	קָלַל
To wait.	יָחַל
To tear.	טָרַף
To be dried up. Be dry.	חָרֵב
To remove. [5 סור]	הֵסִיר
To speak. [3]	דִּבֶּר
To smell. [5 רוח]	הֵרִיחַ
To curse. [3]	קַלֵּל

CHAP. 9.

To seek. Demand.	דָּרַשׁ
To pour. Shed (blood).	שָׁפַךְ
To perish. [2]	הִכָּרֵת
To gather clouds. Speculate on clouds [3] (practice sorcery).	עָנַן
To disperse.	נָפַץ
To drink.	שָׁתָה
To be drunken.	שָׁכֹר
To uncover. Reveal.[1]	גָּלָה
To go.	יָלַךְ
To awake.	יָקַץ
To enlarge. Entice.[2]	פָּתָה

CHAP. 10.

To disperse.	פּוּץ

To be divided. [2 פלג]	הִפָּלֵג

CHAP. 11.

To journey. Move on.[1]	נָסַע
To make bricks.	לָבַן
To burn.	שָׂרַף
To descend.	יָרַד רֶדֶת
To withhold. Cut off[2] (branches). Fortify.[3]	בָּצַר
To devise.	זָמַם
To confound. Mix.	בָּלַל
To cease. Forbear.[4]	חָדַל

CHAP. 12.

לֶךְ לְךָ

To show. [5 ראה]	הַרְאָה
To be, or become great. Grow.	גָּדַל
To acquire.	רָכַשׁ
To remove. [5 עתק]	הֶעְתִּיק
To extend. Incline. [5]	נָטָה. נְטוֹת. הַטּוֹת
To sojourn. Fear.[5]	גּוּר
To come near. Bring near.[6] [5 קרב] Offer.[7]	הִקְרִיב
To be well. Be Good.	יָטַב
To praise. [3]	הַלֵּל

---

[1] Gen. 35: 7. [2] Ex. 22: 15; Deut. 11: 16.

[1] Ex. 14: 19; Num. 10: 33. [2] Lev. 25: 5. [3] Num. 13: 28. [4] Num. 9: 13. [5] Deut. 1: 17. [6] Ex. 29: 1. [7] Lev. 1: 2.

CHAP. 13.

To can. Prevail.[1]	יָכֹל
To turn to the right.	הֵימִין [ימן 5]
To turn to the left.	הַשְׂמְאִיל [שמאל 5]
To set up a tent.	אָהֵל
To number.	מָנָה

CHAP. 14.

To join. Enchant.[2]	חָבֵר
To rebel.	מָרַד
To array. Estimate.[3]	עָרַךְ
To flee.	נוּס
To take as a captive.	שָׁבָה
To draw out (troops). Draw[4] (the sword). [רוק 5] Empty out.[5]	הָרִיק
To pursue.	רָדַף
To divide. Allot.[6]	חָלַק
To deliver. [3]	מַגֵּן
To enrich. [עשר 5]	הֶעֱשִׁיר

CHAP. 15.

To take possession. Expel.[7]	יָרַשׁ. רֶשֶׁת
To look. Behold. [נבט 5]	הִבִּיט
To number.	סְפֹר

To believe. Trust.[1]	הַאֲמִין [אמן 5]
To account. Think.	חָשַׁב
To divide.	בָּתַר
To drive away. [נשב 5]	הִשֵּׁב
To humble. Fornicate.[2] [3]	עָנָה
To bury.	קָבַר
To conclude (a covenant). Cut off.[3] Destroy.	כָּרַת

CHAP. 16.

To restrain. Shut up.	עָצַר
To be lightly esteemed. [קלל 2]	נָקַל
To judge.	שָׁפַט
To flee. Bolt.[4]	בָּרַח

CHAP. 17.

To circumcise.	מוּל / נָמַל
To make void. [פרר 5]	הָפֵר
To laugh. Jest.[5]	צָחַק

CHAP. 18.

וירא

To be warm.	חָמַם
To stand. [2]	נִצַּב
To run.	רוּץ
To prostrate oneself. [שחה 7]	הִשְׁתַּחֲוָה

---

[1] Gen. 30: 8. [2] Deut. 18: 11. [3] Lev. 27: 8. [4] Ex. 15: 9. [5] Geu. 42: 35. [6] Deut. 4: 19. [7] Deut. 2: 12.

[1] Deut. 28: 66. [2] Gen. 34: 2. [3] Ex. 4: 25. [4] Ex. 36: 33. [5] Gen. 19: 14.

To wash oneself.	רָחַץ
To recline.	הִשָּׁעֵן [שען 2]
To sustain.	סָעַד
To hasten.	מַהֵר [3]
To knead.	לוּשׁ
To stand.	עָמַד
To waste. Wear out.[1]	בָּלָה
To be wonderful. Difficult.[2]	הִפְלָא [פלא 2]
To deny. Lie.[3]	כַּחֵשׁ [3]
To look out.	הַשְׁקִיף [שקף 5]
To be Enormous. Dim.[3] Hard.[4]	כָּבֵד
To turn.	פָּנָה
To approach. Recede.[5]	נָגַשׁ גֶּשֶׁת
To destroy. Add.[6]	סָפָה
To begin. Consent.[7]	הוֹאִיל [יאל 5]
To draw near. Depart.	סוּר

CHAP. 19.

To lodge. Remain.[8]	לוּן לִין
To rise early.	הַשְׁכֵּם [שכם 5]
To urge. Press.	פָּצַר

To break. Buy,[1] or sell[2] (food).	שָׁבַר
To bake.	אָפָה
To lie down.	שָׁכַב
To do evil. Sound the trumpet.	הָרַע [רוע 5]
To be weary. Loathsome.[3]	לָאָה
To urge.	אוּץ
To linger.	הִתְמַהְמֵהַּ [מהמה 7]
To take hold. Retain.[4]	הַחֲזִיק [חזק 5]
To compassionate.	חָמַל
To escape.	הִמָּלֵט [מלט 2]

CHAP. 20.

To marry.	בָּעַל
To withhold.	חָשַׂךְ
To approach.	קָרַב
To sin.	חָטָא
To restore. Bring back.	הֵשִׁיב [שוב 5]
To pray.	הִתְפַּלֵל [פלל 7]
To wander.	תָּעָה
To be confronted.	נֹכַח [יכח 2]
To heal.	רָפָא

---

[1] Deut. 8: 4. [2] Deut. 30: 11. [3] Gen. 43: 10. [4] Ex. 9: 7. [5] Gen. 19: 9. [6] Num. 82: 14. [7] Ex. 2: 21. [8] Lev. 19: 13.

[1] Gen. 42: 2. [2] Gen. 41: 66. [3] Ex. 7: 15. [4] Ex. 9: 2.

CHAP. 21.

To visit. Number.[1] Appoint.[2]   פָּקַד

To Speak. [3]   מָלַל

To suck.   יָנַק

To wean. Bestow (good or evil on any one).[3] Ripen.[4]   גָּמַל

To be evil.   יָרַע

To cast. [2 שלך]   הִשְׁלִיךְ

To weep.   בָּכָה

To swear. [5 שבע]   הִשָּׁבַע

To deal falsely.   שָׁקַר

To reprove. Judge.[5] Appoint.[6]   [5 יכח]   הוֹכִיחַ

To take forcibly.   גָּזַל

To set. Erect.[7]   [5 נצב]   הִצִּיב

To dig. Search.[8]   חָפַר

CHAP. 22.

To try. [3]   נִסָּה

To love.   אָהַב

To saddle. Bind on.[9]   חָבַשׁ

To bind.   עָקַד

To slaughter.   שָׁחַט

To take hold of.   אָחַז

To speak.   נָאַם

CHAP. 23.
חיי שרה

To mourn.   סָפַד

To answer. Shout.[1] Speak (with emphasis).   עָנָה

To urge. Meet.[2]   פָּגַע

To weigh.   שָׁקַל

CHAP. 24.

To cause to swear. [5 שבע]   הִשְׁבִּיעַ

To be willing.   אָבָה

To take heed. [2 שמר]   הִשָּׁמֵר

To be clear. Free.[3] [2 נקה]   הִנָּקֵה

To kneel.   בָּרַךְ

To appoint.[4] [5 קרח]   הִקְרֵה

To draw (water).   שָׁאַב

To give to drink. [5 גמא]   הִגְמָא

To bring down. [5 ירד]   הוֹרִיד

To empty. [3]   עָרָה

To look on with astonishment. [7 שאה]   הִשְׁתָּאָה

To be silent. [5 חרש]   הַחֲרִישׁ

To prosper.   צָלַח

[1] Num. 1: 3. [2] Num. 27: 16. [3] Gen. 50: 15. [4] Num. 17: 23. [5] Gen. 31: 37. [6] Gen. 21: 14. [7] Gen. 35: 20. [8] Deut. 1: 22. [9] Ex. 29: 9.

[1] Ex. 32: 18. [2] Gen. 32: 2. [3] Ex. 21: 19. [4] Gen. 44: 29.

To bow down.	קָדַד	To be strong.	עָצַם
To lead.	נָחָה	To encamp.	חָנָה
To clear. [3]	פָּנָה	To strive.	רִיב. רוֹב
To ungird. Engrave.¹ [3]	פָּתַח	To strive. [7 עשק]	הִתְעַשֵּׂק
To delay.	אָחַר	To make spacious. Extend.⁵ [5 רחב]	הַרְחִיב
To ask. Borrow.²	שָׁאַל		
To ride.	רָכַב	To dig. Buy.²	כָּרָה
To meditate.	שׂוּחַ	To hate.	שָׂנֵא
To relate. [3]	סָפַר	To be old. Become old.	זָקֵן

CHAP. 25.

תולדת

CHAP. 27.

To entreat.	עָתַר	To be dim.	כָּהָה
To struggle. [7 רצץ]	הִתְרֹצֵץ	To hunt	צוּד
To be strong.	אָמֵץ	To feel. Depart.³	מוּשׁ
To cook. Act wickedly.³ [5 זיד]	הַזִּיד	To recognize. [5 נכר]	הַכִּיר
To allow to eat greedily. [5 לעט]	הַלְעִיט	To bring near. [5 נגשׁ]	הַגִּישׁ
To sell.	מָכַר	To kiss. Show obedience.⁴	נָשַׁק
To despise.	בָּזָה	To be.	הָוָה

CHAP. 26.

To be long.	אָרַךְ	To tremble.	חָרַד
To envy. Be jealous.⁴ Be zealous.⁵ [3]	קָנָא	To supplant.	עָקַב
To stop up. [3]	סָתַם	To reserve. Separate.⁵	אָצַל
		To sustain. Lay on.⁶	סָמַךְ
		To break off.	פָּרַק
		To hate.	שָׂטַם

---

¹ Ex. 28: 36. ² Ex. 3: 22; 22: 13.
³ Ex. 21: 14. ⁴ Num. 5: 14. ⁵ Num. 25: 11.

¹ Deut. 12: 20. ² Deut. 2: 6. ³ Ex. 13: 22; Num. 14: 44. ⁴ Gen. 41: 40. ⁵ Num. 11: 17. ⁶ Ex. 29: 10.

To forget.	שָׁכַח	To endow.	זָבַד
To be bereaved.	שָׁכֹל	To dwell with.	זָבַל
To be weary. To loathe.	קוּץ	To divine. [3]	נָחֵשׁ

To forget. — שָׁכַח
To be bereaved. — שָׁכֹל
To be weary. To loathe. — קוּץ

CHAP. 28.

וַיֵּצֵא

To reach. [5 נגע] — הִגִּיעַ
To dream. — חָלַם
To spread. Break forth.¹ — פָּרַץ
To pour. Cast.² — יָצַק צֶקֶת
To vow. — נָדַר
To tithe. [3] — עָשַׂר

CHAP. 29.

To roll. — גָּלַל
To pasture. — רָעָה
To embrace. — חָבַק
To give. Procure. — יָהַב
To deceive. [3] — רַמָּה
To join. Borrow.³ — לָוָה
To praise. [5 ידה] — הוֹדוֹת

CHAP. 30.

To withhold. — מָנַע
To wrestle. [2 פתל] — הִפָּתֵל
To call happy. [3] — אִשֵּׁר
To hire. — שָׂכַר

To endow. — זָבַד
To dwell with. — זָבַל
To divine. [3] — נָחֵשׁ
To specify. Blaspheme.¹ — נָקַב
To steal. Deceive.² — גָּנַב
To be left. [2 יתר] — הוֹתֵר
To peel. [3] — פָּצֵל
To make bare. — חָשַׂף
To place. [5 יצג] — הִצִּיג
To be hot. — יָחַם
To separate. Disperse.³ [5 פרד] — הַפְרִיד
To be strong. Bind. — קָשַׁר
To be feeble. [5 עיף] — הֶעֱטִיף

CHAP. 31.

To deceive. [2] — הִתֵּל
To change. — חָלַף
To take away. Deliver. [5 נצל] — הִצִּיל
To anoint. — מָשַׁח
To lead. Drive. — נָהַג
To shear. — גָּזַז
To overtake. [5 דבק] — הַדְבִּיק

---

¹ Gen. 38: 29. ² Ex. 25: 12. ³ Deut. 28: 12.

·¹ Lev. 21: 16. ² Gen. 31: 20. ³ Dout. 32: 7.

7*

78 VERBS.

To reach. Overtake.[1] — הַשִּׂיג [נשג 5]

To pitch (a tent). Blow (a trumpet). Cast away.[2] — תָּקַע

To give leave. Forsake. Scatter.[3] — נָטַשׁ

To act foolishly. — הַשְׂכִּיל [סכל 5]

To long. — הַכָּסֵף [כסף 2]

To search. Grope.[4] — מָשַׁשׁ [3]

To search. — חָפַשׂ

To pursue hotly. — דָּלַק

To abort. Bereave.[5] — שָׁכֵּל [3]

To bear loss. Offer for sins committed.[6] Cleanse.[7] — חַטָּא [3]

To require. Seek. — בַּקֵּשׁ [3]

To depart. — נָרַד

To collect. — לָקַט

To watch. — צָפָה

To cast. Shoot. — יָרָה

To slaughter. — זָבַח

CHAP. 32.

וישלח

To divide. — חָצָה

To be little. Unworthy. — קָטֹן

To meet. — פָּגַשׁ

To appease. Atone. — כָּפַר [3]

To wrestle. — הֵאָבֵק [אבק 2]

To be dislocated. — יָקַע

To contend. — שָׂרָה

To be delivered. Escape. — הִנָּצֵל [נצל 2]

To halt. — צָלַע

CHAP. 33.

To be gracious to. — חָנַן

To receive favorably. Conciliate. Compensate.[1] — רָצָה

To have young. Suckle (of cattle). — עָלוֹת [עול]

To overdrive. — דָּפַק

To lead on. Provide for.[2] — נָהַל

CHAP. 34.

To defile. Declare unclean.[3] — טָמֵא [3]

To delight. — חָשַׁק

To intermarry. — הִתְחַתֵּן [חתן 7]

To traffic. — סָחַר

To settle oneself. — הֵאָחֵז [אחז 2]

To consent. — יָאַת

To delight. — חָפֵץ

---

¹ Deut. 28: 2. ² Ex. 10: 19. ³ Num. 11: 31. ⁴ Deut. 28: 29. ⁵ Gen. 42: 36. ⁶ Lev. 6: 19. ⁷ Num. 19: 19.

¹ Lev. 26: 34. ² Gen. 47: 17. ³ Lev. 13: 3.

To be honored. [2 נכר] הִכָּבֵד

To be sore. כָּאַב

To plunder. בָּזַז

To trouble. עָכַר

To be odious. To stink. בָּאַשׁ

To be destroyed. [2 שמד] הִשָּׁמֵד

CHAP. 35.

To purify oneself. Undergo a course of purification.[1] [7 טהר] הִטַּהֵר

To hide. טָמַן

To pour out (a libation). נָסַךְ

To be difficult. Hard. קָשָׁה

CHAP. 36.

To reign. מָלַךְ

CHAP. 37.

וישב

To bind sheaves. [3] אָלַם

To rebuke. גָּעַר

To conspire. [7 נכל] הִתְנַכֵּל

To slay. Kill. [5 מות] הֵמִית

To strip. [5 פשט] הִפְשִׁיט

To draw. Prolong. מָשַׁךְ

To bring up. Light up.[2] Sacrifice.[3] [5 עלה] הֶעֱלָה

To rend. קָרַע

To dip. טָבַל

To mourn. [7 אבל] הִתְאַבֵּל

To refuse. [3] מָאֵן

CHAP. 38.

To marry a brother's widow. [3] יַבֵּם

To wrap oneself. [7 עלף] הִתְעַלֵּף

To fornicate. Be perfidious. זָנָה

To be righteous. צָדֵק

CHAP. 39.

To serve. Minister unto. [3] שָׁרֵת

To appoint. Deposit.[1] [5 פקד] הִפְקִיד

To bind. Hold in prison. אָסַר

CHAP. 40.

To be angry. קָצַף

To be sad. זָעַף

To interpret. פָּתַר

To ripen. Cook. בָּשַׁל

To squeeze out. שָׂחַט

To hang (trans.). תָּלָה

CHAP. 41.

מקץ

To blast. שָׂדַף

---

[1] Lev. 14: 4. [2] Ex. 25: 37. [3] Lev. 14: 20.

[1] Lev. 5: 23.

To swallow. Cover.[1]   בָּלַע

To be troubled (in spirit).   הִפָּעֵם [2 פעם]

To bring on hastily.   הָרִיץ [5 רוץ]

To shave.   גִּלַּח [3]

To be arid.   צָנַם

To repeat.   שָׁנָה

To be established. Prosper.[2] Prepared.[3]   הֵכוֹן [2 כון]

To take a fifth part. [3]   חַמֵּשׁ

To gather.   קָבַץ

To pile up.   צָבַר

To forget. Claim a debt.[4]   נָשָׁה

To hunger.   רָעֵב

To be, or become strong. Be urgent.[5]   חָזַק

CHAP. 42.

To look at one another.   הִתְרָאָה [7 ראה]

To estrange oneself.   הִתְנַכֵּר [7 נכר]

To prove. Try.   בָּחַן

To beseech.   הִתְחַנֵּן [7 חנן]

To espy.   רַגֵּל [3]

CHAP. 43.

To declare. Call to witness.[1]   הָעִיד [5 עוד]

To be surety.   עָרַב

To slaughter.   טָבַח

To prepare.   הֵכִין [5 כון]

To seek a quarrel.   הִתְגַּלָּל [7 גלל]

To rush upon. Prostrate oneself.[2]   הִתְנַפֵּל [7 נפל]

To be excited.   הִכָּמֵר [2 כמר]

To refrain oneself.   הִתְאַפֵּק [7 אפק]

To marvel.   תָּמַהּ

CHAP. 44.

To be far off.   רָחַק

To requite. Pay.[3]   שָׁלֵם [3]

To lift (a burden).   עָמַס

To justify oneself.   הִצְטַדֵּק [7 צדק]

CHAP. 45.

וִיגַּשׁ

To happen. Meet.[4]   קָרָה

To be terrified.   הִבָּהֵל [2 בהל]

To support.   כִּלְכֵּל [3 כול]

To be impoverished.   הוּרַשׁ [2 ירש]

---

[1] Num. 4: 20. [2] Ex. 8: 22. [3] Ex. 19: 11. [4] Deut. 24: 11. [5] Ex. 12: 13.

[1] Deut. 4: 26. [2] Deut. 9: 18. [3] Ex. 21: 36. [4] Deut. 25: 18.

To load. טָעַן

To pity. חוּס

To quarrel. Tremble.[1] רָגַז

To be frigid. פוּג

CHAP. 46.

To direct. Teach.[2] [ירה 5] הוֹרוֹת

CHAP. 47.

To faint. לָהַהּ

To be at an end. Expire.[3] תָּמַם

To be at an end. אָפֵס

To hide. [3] כָּחַד

To be desolate. שָׁמֵם

To remove. Set apart.[4] [עבר 5] הֶעֱבִיר

CHAP. 48.

וַיְחִי

To be sick. חָלָה

To collect one's strength. Take courage.[5] [חזק 7] הִתְחַזֵּק

To contemplate. [3] פָּלֵל

To traverse. [3] שָׂכֵל

To deliver. Redeem.[6] גָּאַל

To increase as the fishes. דָּגָה

To take hold of. Support.[1] תָּמַךְ

CHAP. 49.

To excel. Let remain.[2] Make pre-eminent.[3] [יתר 5] הוֹתִיר

To profane. [3] חַלֵּל

To be united. יַחַד

To lame. [3] עָקַר

To kneel down. כָּרַע

To wash (garments). [3] כָּבֵּס

To be pleasant. נָעֵם

To bear. סָבַל

To bite. נָשַׁךְ

To hope. [3] קָוָה

To invade. גוּד

To tread. צָעַד

To embitter. מָרַר

To be strong. פָּזַז

To help. עָזַר

CHAP. 50

To embalm. חָנַט

To place. יָשַׂם

---

[1] Deut. 2: 25. [2] Ex. 35: 34. [3] Num. 32: 13. [4] Ex. 13: 12. [5] Num. 13: 20. [6] Lev. 25: 25.

---

[1] Ex. 17: 12. [2] Ex 10: 15. [3] Deut. 28: 11.

EXODUS.

שמות

To be wise.	חָכַם
To fight.	הִלָּחֵם [לחם 2]
To aid in childbirth.	יָלַד [3]

CHAP. 2.

To hide.	צָפַן
To daub.	חָמַר
To place oneself. Stand.	הִתְיַצֵּב [יצב 7]
To carry. Lead.[1]	הוֹלִיךְ [ילך 5]
To draw.	מָשָׁה
To strive.	נִצָּה [2]
To draw (water).	דָּלָה
To help. Save.[5]	הוֹשִׁיעַ [ישע 5]
To sigh.	הֵאָנַח [אנח 2]
To cry out.	זָעַק

CHAP. 3.

To burn.	בָּעַר
To put off. Slip.[2] Cast off.[3] Cast out.[4]	נָשַׁל
To hide.	הִסְתִּיר [סתר 5]
To flow.	זוּב

To oppress. Press.[1]	לָחַץ
To despoil. Strip.[2]	נָצַל [3]

CHAP. 4.

To rejoice.	שָׂמַח
To harden.	חָזַק [3]
To desist. Forsake.[3] Be idle.[4]	רָפָה

CHAP. 5.

To hold a feast.	חָגַג
To disturb.	פָּרַע
To urge.	נָגַשׂ
To gather (straw).	קֹשֵׁשׁ [3]
To diminish. Be less (in importance).[5]	גָּרַע

CHAP. 7.

וארא

To smite. Strike.[6]	נָגַף

CHAP. 8.

To glory oneself.	הִתְפָּאֵר [פאר 7]
To distinguish.	הִפְלָה [פלה 5]
To stone.	סָקַל

CHAP. 9

To sprinkle.	זָרַק

---

[1] Deut. 8: 2. [2] Deut. 19: 5. [3] Deut. 28: 40. [4] Deut. 7: 1.

[1] Num. 22: 25. [2] Ex. 38: 6. [3] Deut. 4: 31. [4] Ex. 5: 8. [5] Num. 9: 7. [6] Ex. 21: 22; 35.

(82)

To break forth.	פָּרַח	To be leavened.	חָמֵץ
To be exterminated.	הֻכְחַד [נחד 2]	To bind up. Insnare.¹ Be hostile to.²	צָרַר
To exalt oneself.	הִסְתּוֹלֵל [סלל 7]	To lend.	הִשְׁאִיל [שאל 5]

To break forth.   פָּרַח

To be exterminated.   הֻכְחַד [נחד 2]

To exalt oneself.   הִסְתּוֹלֵל [סלל 7]

To found.   יָסֹד

To set in safety.   הָעֵין [עין 5]

To inflame.   הִתְלַקַּח [לקח 7]

To spread.   פָּרַשׂ

To pour down (Intrans.).   נִתַּךְ [2]

CHAP. 10.
בא

To mock.   הִתְעַלֵּל [עלל 7]

To perish. Be lost.¹ Wretched.²   אָבַד

To let remain.   הִשְׁאִיר [שאר 5]

To be dark.   חָשַׁךְ

To be stayed.   הֻצַּג [יצג 6]

CHAP. 11.

To sharpen.   חָרַץ

CHAP. 12.

To be little. Few.   מָעַט

To reckon.   כָּסַס

To gird.   חָגַר

To pass over.   פָּסַח

CHAP. 13.

To redeem.   פָּדָה

To break the neck (trans). Drop.³   עָרַף

CHAP. 14.
בשלח

To be entangled. Confused.   הֵבוֹךְ [בוך 2]

To confound. Destroy.   הָמַם

To overthrow.   נָעַר [3]

CHAP. 15.

To sing.   שִׁיר

To be exalted.   גָּאָה

To throw.   רָמָה

To exalt.   רוּם [3]

To glorify.   הִנְוֵה [נוה 5]

To sink.   טָבַע

To be glorious.   נֶאְדָּר [אדר 2]

To crush.   רָעַץ

To overthrow. Break through.⁴   הָרַס

To be heaped up.   הֶעֱרַם [ערם 2]

---

¹ Deut. 22: 3.   ² Deut. 26: 5.

¹ Num. 25: 18.   ² Num. 25: 17.   ³ Deut. 32: 2.   ⁴ Ex. 19: 21.

To congeal.	קָפָא	To select. Behold.[1]	חָזָה
To blow.	נָשַׁף	**CHAP. 19.**	
To sink.	צָלַל	To set bounds.	נָבַל
To melt.	נָמוֹג [כוג 2]	To smoke.	עָשַׁן
To be silent.	דָּמַם	**CHAP. 20.**	
To make. Do.	פָּעַל	To honor.	כַּבֵּד [3]
To establish.	כּוֹנֵן [כון 3]	To murder.	רָצַח
To murmur.	נָלוֹן [לון 2]	To commit adultery.	נָאַף
To be sweet.	כָּתַק	To raise.	הֵנִיף [נוף 5]

CHAP. 16.

CHAP. 21.

משפטים

To murmur.	הָלִין [לין 5]	To pierce.	רָצַע
To be satisfied.	שָׂבַע	To betroth.	יָעַד
To measure.	מָדַד	To deal deceitfully.	בָּגַד
To exceed.	עָדַף	To lie in wait.	צָרְה
To melt.	נָמַס [מסס 2]	To bring to pass.	אָנָה [3]

CHAP. 17.

To thirst.	צָמָא	To amerce.	עָנַשׁ
To discomfit.	חָלַשׁ ●	To gore.	נָגַח

CHAP. 18.

יתרו

CHAP. 22.

To rejoice.	חָרָה	To shine.	זָרַח
To act wickedly.	זוּד	To depasture. Kindle.	הַבְעִיר [בער 5]
To be exhausted.	נָבֵל	To depasture. Kindle.[2] Exterminate.[3]	בָּעַר [3]
To counsel. Predict.[1]	יָעַץ	To declare guilty.	הַרְשִׁיעַ [רשע 5]
To enlighten.	הַזְהִיר [זהר 5]		

---

1 Num. 24: 14.

1 Ex. 24: 11.   2 Ex. 35: 3.   3 Deut. 13: 6.

To betroth.	אָרַשׂ [3]
To purchase (a wife).	מָהֹר
To doom to death, to destruction.¹	הַחֲרִים [חרם 5]
To defraud.	הֹנָיָה [ינה 5]
To lend.	הִלְוָה [לוה 5]
To take as a pledge.	חָבַל

CHAP. 23.

To respect.	הָדַר
To justify.	הִצְדִּיק [צדק 5]
To blind.	עִוֵּר [3]
To pervert.	סִלֵּף [3]
To relinquish.	שָׁמַט
To be refreshed.	הִנָּפֵשׁ [נפש 2]
To rebel.	הֵמֵר [מרר 5]
To be inimical.	אִיב
To be hostile. Form.²	צוּר
To possess. Inherit. Share out.³ Own.⁴	נָחַל

CHAP. 24.

| To write. | כָּתַב |

CHAP. 25.

תרומה

| To impel (to offer). | נָדַב |
| To be red. | אָדֹם |

To overlay.	צִפָּה [3]
To cover.	סָכַךְ
To meet.	נוֹעַד [יעד 2]
To be shaped like almonds.	שֻׁקַּד [4]

CHAP. 26.

To be twined.	הָשְׁזַר [שזר 6]
To be opposite.	הִקְבִּיל [5]
To double.	כָּפַל
To hang over.	סָרַח
To be joined.	שֻׁלַּב [4]
To be coupled.	תָּאַם

CHAP. 27.

| To clear from ashes. | דִּשֵּׁן [3] |
| To hollow. | נָבַב |

CHAP. 28.

תצוה

To minister as a priest.	כִּהֵן [3]
To inclose. Intwine.¹	שָׁבֵץ [3]
To bind on.	רָכַס
To be removed.	הֻזַּח [זחח 2]

CHAP. 29.

To gird on.	אָפַד
To cause to ascend in fumes.	הִקְטִיר [קטר 5]
To dissect.	נָתַח

¹ Deut. 2: 34. ² Ex. 32: 4. ³ Num. 34: 17. ⁴ Ex. 34: 9.

¹ Ex. 28: 39.

8

To sprinkle.	נָזָה	To cover.	שָׂכַךְ

To separate. Offer.[1] Raise erect.[2]   הָרִים [רום 5]

CHAP. 34.

To hew. Carve..   פָּסַל

CHAP. 30.

כי תשא

To keep. Guard.[1]   נָצַר

To pour.   יָסַךְ

To pardon.   סָלַח

To compound.   רָקַח

To break down.   נָתַץ

To be mixed.   מָלַח [4]

To be born a male.   הִזָּכֵר [זכר 2]

To pound.   שָׁחַק

To emit beams (of light).   קָרַן

CHAP. 32.

To delay.   בֹּשֵׁשׁ [בוש 3]

CHAP. 35.

ויקהל

To assemble (intrans).   הִקָּהֵל [קהל 2]

To assemble. (trans).   הִקְהִיל [קהל 5]

To beseech. Afflict.[3]   חַלָּה [3]

To spin.   טָוָה

To engrave.   חָרַת

CHAP. 38.

To grind.   טָחַן

To congregate.   צָבָא

To scatter.   זָרָה

CHAP. 39.

פקודי

CHAP. 33.

To spread out.   רָקַע

To have mercy.   רַחֵם [3]

To cut off.   קָצַץ

Ex. 35: 24.   [2] Gen. 31 : 45.   [3] Deut. 29 : 21.

[1] Deut. 32: 10.

LEVITICUS.

ויקרא

To nip off. מָלַק

To squeeze. מָצָה

To cleave. שָׁסַע

CHAP. 2.

To take a handful. קָמַץ

To break (in morsels). פָּתַת

To salt. מָלַח

To parch. קָלָה

CHAP. 4.

To err. שָׁנָה

To be hidden. [עלם 2] הֶעְלֵם

To be guilty. אָשֵׁם

To pronounce. [3] בִּטֵּא

To confess. [ידה 7] הִתְוַדָּה

To be perfidious. מָעַל

To err. שָׁגַג

To defraud. עָשַׁק

CHAP. 6.

צו

To burn. יָקַד

To put off. פָּשַׁט

To be extinguished. כָּבָה

To be soaked. [רבך 6] הָרְבֵּךְ

To be scoured. [4] מֹרַק

To rinse. שֻׁטַּף

CHAP. 9.

שמיני

To present. [מצא 5] הַמְצִיא

To shout. Rejoice. רָנַן

CHAP. 10.

To rend. פָּרַם

CHAP. 11.

To divide. [פרס 5] הַפְרִיס

To ruminate. גָּרַר

To abominate. Pol-
lute.[1] [3] שָׁקַץ

To leap. [3] נָתַר

To be unclean. Polluted. טָמֵא

To be clean. Pure. טָהֵר

CHAP. 13.

תזריע

To spread. פָּשָׂה

To declare one clean. [3] טָהֵר

To be old. [ישן 2] נוֹשָׁן

To search. [3] בִּקֵּר

To be bald. [מרט 2] הִמָּרֵט

To wrap up. עָטָה

---

[1] Lev. 11 : 43.

(87)

To corrode.	הַמְאִיר [5 מאר]	To be set free.	חָפַשׁ [4]

CHAP. 14.
מצרע

To pull out. Pull off.[1] Draw out (troops).[2]   חָלַץ

To regard as uncircumcised.   עָרַל

To scrape off. { הַקְצִיעַ [5 קצע] / הַקְצָה [5 קצה] }

To go around, (in shaving the head).   הַקִּיף [5 נקף]

To plaster.   טוֹחַ

CHAP. 20.

To stone.   רָגַם

CHAP. 15.

To flow.   רוֹר

To hide.   הֶעֱלִים [5 עלם]

To stop up.   הַחְתִּים [5 חתם]

To make bare.   הֶעֱרָה [5 ערה]

To spit.   רָקַק

CHAP. 21.
אמר

To separate.   הַזִּיר [5 נזר]

To make bald.   קָרַח

CHAP. 16.
אחרי מות

To cut one's flesh.   שָׂרַט

To wrap around, (as a turban).   צָנַף

CHAP. 22.

To abstain.   הַנְזֵר [2 נזר]

CHAP. 18.

To cross the breed, (of different genera).   רָבַע

To specify.   פִּלֵּא [3]

To vomit.   קוֹא

CHAP. 24.

To declare.   פָּרַשׁ

CHAP. 19.
קדושים

CHAP. 25.
בהר

To mow. Be short.[3]   קָצַר

To prune.   זָמַר

To glean.   עָלַל

To be reduced to poverty.   מוּךְ

To totter.   מוֹט

To retain (a grudge)   נָטַר

CHAP. 26.
בחקתי

To loathe.   גָּעַל

To give up.   חָרַף

To despise.   מָאַס

To pine away.   דָּאַב

---

[1] Deut. 25: 9.   [2] Num. 31: 3; compare [5 חלץ] page 73, Col. A.   [3] Num. 11: 23.

To chastise. [3] יַסֵּר	To be humbled. [2 כנע] הִכָּנַע
To destroy. [5 שמד] הִשְׁמִיד	To specify. Make distinguished.[1] [5 פלא] הִפְלִיא
To be driven on. [2 נדף] הִנָּדֵף	To exchange. [5 מור] הֵמִיר
To pine away. [2 מקק] נָמֹק	To be first born. [4] בָּכַר

NUMBERS.

במדבר

To be registered on a genea- [7 ילד] הִתְיַלֵּד
logical table.

CHAP. 5.
נשא

To turn aside. שָׂטָה

To swell. צָבָה

CHAP. 9.
בהעלתך

To be taken up. [2 עלה] הֵעָלוֹת

CHAP. 10.

To be delivered. [2 ישע] נוֹשַׁע

To do good. [5 טוב] הֵיטִיב

To search out. תּוּר

CHAP. 11.

To complain. [7 אנן] הִתְאוֹנֵן

To subside. שָׁקַע

To lust. [7 אוה] הִתְאַוָּה

To go about. שׁוּט

To pound. דּוּךְ

To prophesy. [7 נבא] הִתְנַבֵּא

To bring on. גּוּז

To spread out. שָׁטַח

CHAP. 12.

To act foolishly. [2 יאל] נוֹאַל

To spit. יָרֹק

To be ashamed. [2 כלם] הִכָּלֵם

CHAP. 13.
שלח לך

To still. [5] הָסָה

CHAP. 14.

To despise. נָאֵץ

To act presump- [5 עפל] הֶעְפִּיל
tuously.

To crush. כָּתַת

CHAP. 15.

To insult. [3] גָּדַף

---

¹ Deut. 29: 59.

8*

CHAP. 16.

קרח

To assume dominion. הִשְׂתָּרֵר [שׂרר 7]

To pick out (the eyes). נָקֵר [3]

CHAP. 17.

To get away. הָרֵם [רום 2]

To blossom. צוץ

CHAP. 19.

חקת

To have oneself purified. הִתְחַטֵּא [חבא 7]

CHAP. 20.

To rebel. מָרָה

CHAP. 21.

To capture. לָכַד

CHAP. 22.

בלק

To liek up. לָחַךְ

To curse. קָבַב

To draw out. שָׁלַף

To be accustomed. הַסְכִּין [סכן 5]

To be perverse. יָרַט

CHAP. 23.

To let out one's anger. זָעַם

To behold. שׁוּר

To be false. כָּזַב [3]

To be right. Pleasing. יָשַׁר

CHAP. 24.

To be open. שָׁתַם

To flow. נָזַל

To crush (bones). גָּרַם [3]

To shatter. Bruise.[1] מָחַץ

To clap. סָפַק

To tread. דָּרַךְ

To destroy. קַרְקַר [קור 3]

CHAP. 25.

To adhere to. נִצְמַד [צמד 2]

To hang (trans). הוֹקִיעַ [יקע 5]

To pierce. דָּקַר

פנחס

To plot. נָכַל [3]

CHAP. 30.

מטות

To restrain. הֵנִיא [נוא 5]

CHAP. 31.

To separate. Turn aside.[2] מָסַר

CHAP. 33.

מסעי

To destroy. Lay waste. אָבֵד [3]

To intend. דָּמָה [3]

CHAP. 34.

To mark out. תָּאָה [3]

CHAP. 35.

To thrust. Expel. הָדַף

To pollute. חָנַף

---

[1] Deut. 32: 39.   [2] Num. 31: 16.

DEUTERONOMY.

דברים

To explain.	[3] בָּאֵר
To be discouraged.	נָחַת [נחת 2]
To murmur.	נִרְגָּן [רגן 2]
To dread.	עָרִץ
To be angry.	אָנַף
To be rash.	[5] הוּן

CHAP. 2.

To contend.	הִתְגָּרֶה [גרה 7]
To tremble.	חוּל
To be lofty.	שָׂגַב

CHAP. 3.

ואתחנן

| To be in anger. | הִתְעַבֵּר [עבר 7] |

CHAP. 4.

To teach.	[3] לַמֵּד
To learn.	לָמַד
To impel. Drive on.	נָדַח
To be angry.	כָּעַס

CHAP. 6.

| To inculcate. | [3] שָׁנֵן |
| To hew. | חָצַב |

CHAP. 7.

| To cut down. Break in pieces.[1] | [3] גָּדַע |

עקב

| To be ensnared. | נֹקַשׁ [יקשׁ 2] |
| To abhor. | [3] תָּעַב |

CHAP. 8.

| To swell. | בָּצֵק |

CHAP. 9.

| To subdue. | הַכְנִיעַ [כנע 5] |
| To fear. | יָגֹר |

CHAP. 11.

| To cause to over-flow. | הֵצִיף [צוף 5] |

CHAP. 13.

ראה

To seduce. Drive out.[2]	הַדִּיחַ [נדח 5]
To entice.	הֵסִית [סות 5]
To search.	חָקֹר

CHAP. 14.

To cut oneself.	הִתְגֹּדֵד [גדד 7]
To lend.	הֶעֱבִיט [עבט 5]
To borrow. Give or take[3] a pledge.	עָבֹט
To shut.	קָפַץ

---

[1] Deut. 12: 3.   [2] Deut. 30: 1.   [3] Deut. 24: 10.

(91)

To give liberally. [עֶנֶק 5] הַעֲנִיק

CHAP. 18.
שפטים

To divine. · קָסַם

CHAP. 19.

To divide in three. [3] שִׁלֵּשׁ

To hew. חָטַב

To lie in wait. אָרַב

To remove. [נסג 5] הַסִּיג

CHAP. 20.

To be timid. Be tender. רָכַךְ

To flee hastily. חָפַז

To dedicate. חָנַךְ

To make peace. [שלם 5] הִשְׁלִים

CHAP. 21.
כי תצא

To act as master. [עמר 7] הִתְעַמֵּר

To consider as firstborn. [3] בִּכֵּר

To be stubborn. סָרַר

To be gluttonous. זָלַל

To drink excessively. כָּבָא

CHAP. 22.
To plow. חָרַשׁ

CHAP. 23.
To wound. פָּצַע

To come to aid. [3] קָדַם

To take usury. [נשך 5] הִשִּׁיךְ

To pluck. קָטַף

CHAP. 24.
To beat off. חָבַט

To glean. [3] פָּאַר

CHAP. 25.
To be despicable. [קלה 2] נִקְלָה

To muzzle. חָסַם

To thresh. · דּוּשׁ

To smite the hindmost. [3] זִנֵּב

CHAP. 26.
כי תבוא
To avouch. [אמר 5] הֶאֱמִיר

CHAP. 27.
To plaster. שׂוּד

To be attentive. [סכת 5] הַסְכֵּת

CHAP. 28.
To lie with. שָׁגַל

To crush. רָצַץ

To cat off. חָסַל

To gather. אָגַר

To anoint. סוּךְ

To consume. [3] יָרַשׁ

To fly swiftly. דָּאָה

To besiege. [צרר 5] הֵצַר

To trust. בָּטַח

To distress.	[5 צוק] הָצִיק	To kindle.	קָדַח
To live delicately.	[7 ענג] הִתְעַנֵּג	To set on fire.	[3] לָהַט
To rejoice.	שׂוּשׂ	To devour.	לָחַם
To be plucked up.	[2] נִסַּח	To crawl.	זָחַל
To be at ease.	[5 רגע] הִרְגִּיעַ	To exterminate	[5 פאה] הִפְאָה
To hang up.	תָּלָא	To ignore.	[3] נִכֵּר
To fear.	פָּחַד	To lay up.	כָּמַס

CHAP. 29.

נצבים

To pluck up.	נָתַשׁ	To seal up.	חָתַם
		To hasten.	חוּשׁ

CHAP. 31.

וילך

To be fat.	דָּשֵׁן	To fail.	אָזַל
		To take refuge.	חָסָה
		To sharpen.	שָׁנַן

CHAP. 32.

האזינו

CHAP. 33.

הברכה

To consider. Regard.¹	בִּין	To shine brightly.	[5 יפע] הוֹפִיעַ
To stir up.	[5 עור] הֵעִיר	To come.	אָתָה
To be fat.	שָׁמֵן	To love.	חָבַב
To kick.	בָּעַט	To be prostrated.	[4] תֻּכָּה
To be thick.	עָבָה	To shield.	חָפָה
To be fleshy.	כָּשָׂה	To hide.	שָׂפַן / סָפַן
To despise.	[3] נָבֵל	To leap.	[3] זָנַק
To fear.	שָׂעַר	To fawn.	[2 כחש] הִתְכַּחֵשׁ

¹ Deut. 32: 10.

PARTICLES;

Including Adjectives and other parts of Speech not given in the preceding lists, except the Pronouns and Numerals.

GENESIS.

בראשית

	אֶת*
Waste.	תֹהוּ
Void.	בֹהוּ
Upon. Over. Near.	עַל
That. For. Because. When.	כִּי
Good.	טוֹב
Between. Among.	בֵּין
That. What. Who. Which.	אֲשֶׁר
Under. Instead of. Because.[1]	תַּחַת

---

* The word as used here, and as it most frequently occurs, cannot be properly translated by any word of the same import. It is to be regarded as a preposition, mostly used before nouns in the objective case, though often also before the nominative. Its origin and signification appears doubtful to the Hebrew grammarians. Sometimes it stands for *with*, and as such will be found in its proper place.

[1] Deut. 4: 37; 21: 14.

(94)

So. Thus. Rightly.[1] Honest.[2]	כֵּן
To.	אֶל
Great. Large. Elder.	גָּדוֹל
Small. Younger.	{ קָטוֹן / קָטָן
Living.	חַי
All. Every. Any.	{ כֹּל / כָּל-
Behold.	הִנֵּה
Very. Very much.	מְאֹד

CHAP. 2.

These.	אֵלֶּה
Not yet.	טֶרֶם
Not. No.	לֹא

---

[1] Ex. 10: 29.   [2] Gen. 42: 11.

There is not. Was not.	אֵין	Not to.	לְבִלְתִּי
From.	מִן	With me.	עִמָּדִי
There.	שָׁם ׁ. שָׁמָּה	For the sake of. In order that.	בַּעֲבוּר
Desirable.	נֶחְמָד	Until. Unto.	עַד
That. This. That is. { m. / f.	הוּא / הִיא	Behold.	הֵן
Alone. Besides.	לְבַד	Now.	עַתָּה
Over against.	כְּנֶגֶד		

CHAP. 4.

What. How.[1] Why.[2] {	מָה / מֶה	With.	אֵת
		If. Whether.	אִם
		Where.	אִי
This. That. That is. { f. / m.	זֹאת / זֶה	Therefore.	לָכֵן
		Before.	לִפְנֵי
Therefore. Since.	עַל־כֵּן	Again. More. Yet.	עוֹד
Naked.	עָרֹם	Another.	אַחֵר
		Then.	אָז

CHAP. 3.

CHAP. 5.

Subtle.	עָרוּם	After. Behind. {	אַחֲרֵי / אַחַר
Even. Also.	אַף		
Lest.	פֶּן	Not.	אֵין
Also.	גַּם		

CHAP. 6.

With.	עִם	Since also.	בְּשַׁגַּם
Naked.	עֵירֹם	Great. Much. Enough.	רַב
Where.	אַיֵּה	Only. Surely.[1] Lean.[2]	רַק
Who.	מִי	Evil. Bad. Sad.[3]	רַע

---

[1] Gen. 28: 17.   [2] Ex. 14: 15.

[1] Gen. 20: 11.   [2] Gen. 41: 19.   [3] Gen. 40: 7.

	נח	Beautiful.	יָפֶה
Upright. Perfect.	תָּמִים	Because of. In order that.	לְמַעַן
On account of. From before.	מִפְּנֵי	For the sake of.	בִּגְלַל
		Why.	לָמָה

CHAP. 7.

Righteous. צַדִּיק

Clean. Pure. טָהוֹר

Self-same. עֶצֶם

About. For. בְּעַד

High. גָּבֹהַּ

Above. לְמַעְלָה

Only. But. Surely.¹ אַךְ

CHAP. 8.

Pleasant. נִיחֹחַ

CHAP. 9.

Backward. אֲחֹרַנִּית / אָחוֹר

CHAP. 11.

The same. A few. אֲחָדִים

Come on. הָבָה

Barren. עָקָר

CHAP. 12.

לֶךְ לְךָ

Grievous. Heavy. Rich. כָּבֵד

I pray. Raw.² נָא

Beautiful. יָפֶה

Because of. In order that. לְמַעַן

For the sake of. בִּגְלַל

Why. לָמָה

CHAP. 13.

Together. יַחְדָּו

Not. אַל

Irrigated. מַשְׁקֶה

CHAP. 14.

Most High. Uppermost. עֶלְיוֹן

Not to. Without. בִּלְעֲדֵי

CHAP. 15.

Much. הַרְבֵּה

Childless. עֲרִירִי

But. Unless.¹ כִּי־אִם

So. Thus. Here.² There.³ Now.⁴ כֹּה

Three years old. מְשֻׁלָּשׁ

Opposite to. Towards. לִקְרַאת

Full. Perfect. Peaceable. שָׁלֵם

Hitherto. עַד־הֵנָּה

CHAP. 16.

Perhaps. Unless.⁵ אוּלַי

Whence. אֵי־מִזֶּה

---

¹ Gen. 27 : 44.   ² Ex. 12 : 9.

¹ Gen. 32: 27.   ² Gen. 31: 37.   ³ Ex. 2: 12.   ⁴ Ex. 7: 16.   ⁵ Num. 22: 33.

Whither.	אָנָה	Come on.	לְכָה

CHAP. 20.

In truth.			אָמְנָה

CHAP. 21.

Pregnant.	הָרָה	Because of. Concerning.	עַל־אֹדֹת
Here. Hither.	הֲלֹם	Far off.	הַרְחֵק

CHAP. 17.

Almighty.	שַׁדַּי	Here. Hither.	הֵנָּה
Would it were. If it were.	לוּ	Except. Without.	בִּלְתִּי

CHAP. 22.

Verily.	אֲבָל	Far off.	רָחוֹק

CHAP. 18.

 וירא

		Above.	מִמַּעַל
Tender.	רַךְ	Any thing.	מְאוּמָה
Old.	זָקֵן	Only.	יָחִיד
Indeed.	אָמְנָם	Because.	יַעַן
Mighty.	עָצוּם	Because.	עֵקֶב
There is. It is. Was.	יֵשׁ		
Far be it.	חָלִלָה		

CHAP. 23.

חיי שרה

CHAP. 19.

These.	הָאֵל	Full.	מָלֵא
Thither.	הָלְאָה	Round about.	סָבִיב

CHAP. 24.

Here.	פֹּה	Or.	אוֹ
As. Like.	כְּמוֹ	This.	הַלָּזֶה

CHAP. 25.

Near.	קָרוֹב	Satisfied.	שָׂבֵעַ

תולדת

Elder.	בְּכוֹר	In behalf of. Opposite to.	לְנֶכַד
Younger.	צָעִיר		

9

Red.	אַדְמוֹנִי	Spotted.	טָלוּא
Upright.	תָּם	Brown.	חוּם
Faint.	עָיֵף	Striped.	עָקֹד
Red.	אָדֹם	White.	לָבָן
CHAP. 26.		Fresh.	לַח
How.	אֵיךְ	Feeble.	עָטוּף
Almost.	כִּמְעַט		
Why.	מַדּוּעַ	Strong.	קָשׁוּר
CHAP. 27.		**CHAP. 31.**	
Hairy.	שָׂעִיר	The day before yesterday.	שִׁלְשׁוֹם
Smooth.	חָלָק	Grizzled.	בָּרֹד
Costly.	חָמוּד	In that not.	עַל־בְּלִי
Then.	אֵפוֹא	Were it not.	לוּלֵי / לוּלֵא
Bitter.	מַר		
Is it therefore?	הֲכִי	Empty.	רֵיקָם
CHAP. 28.		**CHAP. 33.**	
וַיֵּצֵא		וַיִּשְׁלַח	
Surely.	אָכֵן	Latter. Last. Western.[1]	אַחֲרֹן
Fearful.	נוֹרָא	**CHAP. 34.**	
However.	אוּלָם	Large.	רָחָב
CHAP. 29.		Safely.	בֶּטַח
Whence.	מֵאַיִן	**CHAP. 37.**	
For naught.	חִנָּם	וַיֵּשֶׁב	
CHAP. 30.		Where.	אֵיפֹה
When.	מָתַי	Hence. Here.[2] There.[2]	מִזֶּה
Speckled.	נָקֹד		

---

[1] Deut. 11: 24.　　[2] Num. 22: 24.

Empty. Vain.[1]	רַק		CHAP. 43.
		I pray.	בִּי

CHAP. 38.

Here. — בָּזֶה

CHAP. 47.

וַיִּגַּשׁ

CHAP. 39.

Beside. — אֵצֶל

How many. — כַּמָּה

Few. Little. — מְעַט

CHAP. 41.

מְקֵץ

Fat. — בְּרִיא

According to. — לְפִי

Lo. — הָא

Lean. Fine. Emaciated.[2] — דַּק

Poor. — דַּל

וַיְחִי

Right (not left). — יָמִין

Certain. Proper. Prepared.[3] — נָכוֹן

CHAP. 49.

Discreet. — נָבוֹן

Fierce. Strong. — עַז

Wise. — חָכָם

Red. — חַכְלִילִי

Second. Double. — מִשְׁנֶה

Fat. — שָׁמֵן

By order of. According to. — עַל-פִּי

CHAP. 50.

I pray. — אָנָּא

EXODUS.

שמות

New. — חָדָשׁ

Hard. — קָשֶׁה

CHAP. 2.

Strange. — נָכְרִי

CHAP. 3.

Holy. — קֹדֶשׁ

CHAP. 4.

Leprous. — מְצֹרָע

Dumb. — אִלֵּם

Deaf. — חֵרֵשׁ

[1] Deut.: 32 47. [2] Lev· 21: 20. [3] Ex. 19: 11.

Open (of the eyes).	פָּקֵחַ	Because not.	מִבְּלִי
Blind.	עִוֵּר		
		CHAP. 15.	
CHAP. 5.		Glorious.	נֶאְדָּר
Idle.	נִרְפֶּה	Right.	יָשָׁר
Strong.	חָזָק	**CHAP. 16.**	
		Peeled.	מְחֻסְפָּס
CHAP. 6.		What.	מָן
וארא		According to.	כְּפִי
Uncircumcised.	עָרֵל	How long.	עַד־אָנָה
CHAP. 9.			
Slow of growth.	אָפִיל	**CHAP. 17.**	
		Steady.	אֱמוּנָה
CHAP. 10.			
בא		**CHAP. 18.**	
Eastern.	קָדִים	**יתרו**	
Western.	יָם	Before. Over against.	מוּל
CHAP. 12.		**CHAP. 20.**	
Roasted.	צָלִי	Jealous.	קַנָּא
Sodden.	בָּשֵׁל	Smoking.	עָשֵׁן
Thus.	כָּכָה	**CHAP. 21.**	
		משפטים	
Leavened.	חָמֵץ	Free.	חָפְשִׁי
CHAP. 13.		Goring.	נַגָּח
בשלח		**CHAP. 22.**	
Armed.	חָמֻשׁ	Alive.	חַיִּים
CHAP. 14.		Torn (of beasts).	טְרֵפָה
Entangled.	נָבוֹךְ	Poor.	עָנִי
Chosen.	בָּחוּר	**CHAP. 23.**	
High.	רָם	False.	שָׁוְא

Poor.	אֶבְיוֹן		תִּשָּׂא
CHAP. 25.		Rich.	עָשִׁיר
תרומה		Excellent.	רֹאשׁ
Hammered.	מִקְשָׁה	Pure.	דְּרוֹר
Near by.	לְעֻמַּת		
Almond-shaped.	מְשֻׁקָּד	Sweet smelling.	בֶּשֶׂם / בֹּשֶׂם
CHAP. 26.			
Outermost.	קִיצוֹן	Mixed.	מְמֻלָּח
Middle.	תִּיכֹן	Fine.	הָדֵק
CHAP. 27.		**CHAP. 32.**	
Four-square.	רָבוּעַ	Quickly.	מַהֵר
Hollow.	נָבוּב	Engraven.	חָרוּת
תצוה		Bewildered.	פָּרוּעַ
Pure.	זַךְ	**CHAP. 34.**	
Beaten.	כָּתִית	Merciful.	רַחוּם
CHAP. 28.		Gracious.	חַנּוּן
Doubled.	כָּפוּל	Long.	אֶרֶךְ
Continually.	תָּמִיד	**CHAP. 35.**	
CHAP. 29.		ויקהל	
Holy.	קָדְשׁ	Liberal.	נָדִיב
CHAP. 30.		Enough.	דַי
Strange. Profane.	זַר		

9*

LEVITICUS.

CHAP. 4. וִיקְרָא		Leprous.	צָרוּעַ
Anointed.	מָשִׁיחַ	Torn.	פָּרוּם
CHAP. 5.		Alone.	בָּדָד
Unclean.	טָמֵא	Greenish.	יְרַקְרַק
CHAP. 6. צַו		Fretting.	מַמְאִיר
Entirely.	כָּלִיל	**CHAP. 15.** מְצֹרָע	
CHAP. 7.		Flowing.	זָב
Dry.	חָרֵב	Sick.	דָּוֶה
Abominable.	פִּגּוּל	**CHAP. 16.** אַחֲרֵי מוֹת	
CHAP. 10. שְׁמִינִי		Ready.	עִתִּי
Unholy.	חֹל	Desolate.	גְּזֵרָה
Inside.	פְּנִימָה	**CHAP. 20.** קְדוֹשִׁים	
CHAP. 13. תַזְרִיעַ		Unclean. Abominable.	נִדָּה
Deep.	עָמֹק	**CHAP. 21.** אֱמוֹר	
Reddish.	אֲדַמְדָּם	Lame.	פִּסֵּחַ
Low.	שָׁפָל	Flat-nosed.	חָרֻם
Pale.	כֵּהָה	Extended.	שָׂרוּעַ
Yellow..	צָהֹב	Crook-backed.	גִּבֵּן
Black.	שָׁחֹר	Crushed.	מְרוֹחַ
Bald.	קֵרֵחַ	**CHAP. 22.**	
Bald on the front part of the head.	גִּבֵּחַ	Broken.	שָׁבוּר

(102)

Maimed. חָרוּץ
Having wens. יַבֶּלֶת
Contracted. קָלוֹט
Bruised. מָעוּךְ
Crushed. כָּתוּת
Disjointed. נָתוּק
Cut. כָּרוּת

CHAP. 23.
Beautiful. הָדָר
Interwoven. עֲבֹת

CHAP. 25.
בהר
Old. יָשָׁן
Sufficient for. According to. כְּדֵי

NUMBERS.

במדבר
Upwards. מַעֲלָה

CHAP. 4.
Purple. אַרְגָּמָן

CHAP. 5.
נשא
Besides.. מִבַּלְעֲדֵי
Amen. אָמֵן

CHAP. 6.
Dry. יָבֵשׁ

CHAP. 7.
Covered. צָב

CHAP. 12.
בהעלתך
Meek. עָנָו

Faithful. Constant.[1] נֶאֱמָן

CHAP. 13.
שלח לך
Weak. רָפֶה
Lean. רָזֶה
However. No more.[2] אֶפֶס
Fortified. בָּצוּר

CHAP. 14.
Because not. מִבִּלְתִּי

CHAP. 17.
קרח
Quickly. מְהֵרָה

CHAP. 21.
חקת
Despicable. קְלֹקֵל

[1] Deut. 28 : 59. [2] Deut. 32 : 36.

Wo. Alas.	אוֹי	Unclosed.	גְּלוּי
CHAP. 22. בלק		By.	עָלַי
Narrow.	צָר	Unto.	עָדִי
CHAP. 23.		**CHAP. 32.** מטות	
Alone.	לְבַדְּךָ		
Come on.	לְךָ	Readily.	חוּשׁ
CHAP. 24.		Equipped.	חָלוּץ
Open.	שְׁתָם		

DEUTERONOMY.

דברים		**CHAP. 16.**	
Opposite.	מוּל	Joyful.	שָׂמֵחַ
How.	אֵיכָה	**CHAP. 21.** שפטים	
Except. Only.	זוּלָתִי	Hard.	אֵיתָן
CHAP. 4. ואתחנן		כי תצא	
From.	לְמִן	Stubborn.	סוֹרֵר
Without.	בִּבְלִי	Rebellious.	מֹרֶה
CHAP. 9. עקב		**CHAP. 22.**	
Well.	הֵיטֵב	Strayed.	נִדָּח
CHAP. 13. ראה		**CHAP. 25.**	
Worthless.	בְּלִיָּעַל	Weary.	יָגֵעַ
True.	אֱמֶת	**CHAP. 28.** כי תבא	
		Smitten.	נִגָּף
		Oppressed.	עָשׁוּק

Robbed.	גָּזוּל	Crooked.	פְּתַלְתֹּל
Crushed.	רָצוּץ	Foolish.	נָבָל
Mad.	מְשֻׁגָּע	Wasted.	מָזֶה
Delicate.	עָנֹג	Consumed.	לְחֻם
Trembling.	רַגֵּז	Bitter.	מְרִירִי מָרֹר

CHAP. 30.

נצבים

Hidden.	נִפְלֵא	Fierce.	אַכְזָר

CHAP. 32.

האזינו

CHAP. 33.

הברכה

Perverse.	עִקֵּשׁ	Together.	יַחַד

PRONOUNS.

PERSONAL.

I.	$\left\{ \begin{array}{l} \text{אֲנִי} \\ \text{אָנֹכִי} \end{array} \right.$	We.	אֲנַחְנוּ
Thou.	$\left\{ \begin{array}{l} \text{m. אַתָּה} \\ \text{f. אַתְּ} \end{array} \right.$	Ye.	$\left\{ \begin{array}{l} \text{m. אַתֶּם} \\ \text{f. אַתֵּן} \end{array} \right.$
He.	הוּא	They.	$\left\{ \begin{array}{l} \text{m. הֵם} \\ \text{f. הֵן} \end{array} \right.$
She.	הִיא		

DEMONSTRATIVE.

	Fem.	*Masc.*
This. That.	$\left\{ \begin{array}{l} \text{זֹאת or הַזֹּאת} \\ \text{הִיא or הַהִיא} \end{array} \right.$	$\left\{ \begin{array}{l} \text{זֶה or הַזֶּה} \\ \text{הוּא or הַהוּא} \end{array} \right.$
These. Those.	הֵן or הָהֵן	$\left\{ \begin{array}{l} \text{אֵלֶּה or הָאֵלֶּה} \\ \text{הֵם or הָהֵם} \end{array} \right.$

RELATIVE.

Who. Which. That. What.　　(As a prefix שֶׁ), אֲשֶׁר

INTERROGATIVE.

Who.　　　　　　　　מִי

What. How.　　　　מָה

For POSSESSIVE PRONOUNS see pages 15 and 16.

(106)

Table of personal pronouns formed from prepositions, or their fragments, with pronominal terminations, representing different relations of cases. (See page 16).

Singular.

	Com.	Masc.	Fem.	Masc.	Fem.
	Me.	Thee.	Thee.	Him.	Her.
	אֹתִי	אֹתְךָ	אֹתָךְ	אֹתוֹ	אֹתָהּ
To, or for	לִי	לְךָ	לָךְ	לוֹ	לָהּ
From	מִמֶּנִּי	מִמְּךָ	מִמֵּךְ	מִמֶּנּוּ	מִמֶּנָּה
In	בִּי	בְּךָ	בָּךְ	בּוֹ	בָּהּ
Like	כָּמוֹנִי	כָּמוֹךָ	כָּמוֹךְ	כָּמוֹהוּ	כָּמוֹהָ

Relations: To, or for me / thee / him / her. From me / thee / him / her. In me / in thee / in him / in her. Like me / like thee / like him / like her.

Plural.

	Com.	Masc.	Fem.	Masc.	Fem.
	Us.	You.	You.	Them.	Them.
	אֹתָנוּ	אֶתְכֶם	אֶתְכֶן	אֶתְהֶם	אֶתְהֶן
To, or for	לָנוּ	לָכֶם	לָכֶן	לָהֶם	לָהֶן
From	מִמֶּנּוּ	מִכֶּם	מִכֶּן	מֵהֶם	מֵהֶן
In	בָּנוּ	בָּכֶם	בָּכֶן	בָּהֶם	בָּהֶן
Like	כָּמוֹנוּ	כָּכֶם	כָּכֶן	כָּהֶם	כָּהֶן

Relations: To, or for us / you / them. From us / you / them. In us / in you / in them. Like us / like you / like them.

Some of these pronouns are apt to receive an additional mute, or assume somewhat a different form. In the above table they are represented as they most frequently occur.

NUMERALS.

Cardinal numbers, from one to twenty, admit of gender, but from twenty and upwards they are common to both genders. From one to ten inclusive, they assume also a constructive form, which does not, however, alter their signification.

CARDINAL NUMBERS.

	Fem.		Masc.	
	CONSTRUCTED	ABSOLUTE	CONSTRUCTED	ABSOLUTE
One.	אַחַת	אֶחָת	אַחַד	אֶחָד
Two.	שְׁתֵּי / שְׁתַּיִם	שְׁתַּיִם	שְׁנֵי / שְׁנַיִם	שְׁנַיִם
Three.	שְׁלֹשׁ	שָׁלֹשׁ	שְׁלֹשֶׁת	שְׁלֹשָׁה
Four.	—	אַרְבַּע	אַרְבַּעַת	אַרְבָּעָה
Five.	חֲמֵשׁ	חָמֵשׁ	חֲמֵשֶׁת	חֲמִשָּׁה
Six.	שֵׁשׁ	שֵׁשׁ	שֵׁשֶׁת	שִׁשָּׁה
Seven.	שְׁבַע	שֶׁבַע	שִׁבְעַת	שִׁבְעָה
Eight.	—	שְׁמֹנֶה	שְׁמוֹנַת	שְׁמֹנָה
Nine.	תְּשַׁע	תֵּשַׁע	תִּשְׁעַת	תִּשְׁעָה
Ten.	—	עֶשֶׂר	עֲשֶׂרֶת	עֲשָׂרָה

(108)

	Fem.	*Masc.*
Eleven.	אַחַת עֶשְׂרֵה	אַחַד עָשָׂר
Twelve.	שְׁתֵּים עֶשְׂרֵה	שְׁנֵים עָשָׂר
Thirteen.	שְׁלֹשׁ עֶשְׂרֵה	שְׁלֹשָׁה עָשָׂר
Fourteen.	אַרְבַּע עֶשְׂרֵה	אַרְבָּעָה עָשָׂר
Fifteen.	חֲמֵשׁ עֶשְׂרֵה	חֲמִשָּׁה עָשָׂר
Sixteen.	שֵׁשׁ עֶשְׂרֵה	שִׁשָּׁה עָשָׂר
Seventeen.	שְׁבַע עֶשְׂרֵה	שִׁבְעָה עָשָׂר
Eighteen.	שְׁמֹנֶה עֶשְׂרֵה	שְׁמֹנָה עָשָׂר
Nineteen.	תְּשַׁע עֶשְׂרֵה	תִּשְׁעָה עָשָׂר
Twenty.	. . . . . .	עֶשְׂרִים
Twenty-one.	. . . . .	אֶחָד וְעֶשְׂרִים
Twenty-two.	. . . . .	שְׁנַיִם וְעֶשְׂרִים
Twenty-three.	. . . .	שְׁלֹשָׁה וְעֶשְׂרִים
Thirty.	. . . . .	שְׁלֹשִׁים
Forty.	. . . . .	אַרְבָּעִים
Fifty.	. . . . . .	חֲמִשִּׁים
Sixty.	. . . . . .	שִׁשִּׁים
Seventy.	. . . . . .	שִׁבְעִים
Eighty.	. . . . . .	שְׁמֹנִים
Ninety.	. . . . . .	תִּשְׁעִים
One Hundred.	. . . .	מֵאָה Const. מְאַת
Two Hundred.	. . . . .	מָאתַיִם
Three Hundred.	. . . . .	שְׁלֹשׁ מֵאוֹת
One Thousand.	. . . . .	אֶלֶף

10

Two Thousand.	.	.	.	.		.	.	אַלְפַּיִם
Three Thousand.	.	.	.		.	.	שְׁלשֶׁת אֲלָפִים
Ten Thousand.	.	.	.		רִבּוֹא. עֲשֶׂרֶת אֲלָפִים
Twenty Thousand.	.	.	.		.	.	רִבּוֹאתַיִם
Thirty Thousand.	.	.	.		.	שְׁלִשׁ רִבּוֹא
Hundred Thousand.	.	.	.		.	מֵאַת אֶלֶף
A Million.	.	.	.		.	אֶלֶף אֲלָפִים

ORDINAL NUMBERS.

	Fem.	*Masc.*
First.	רִאשׁוֹנָה	רִאשׁוֹן
Second.	שֵׁנִית	שֵׁנִי
Third.	שְׁלִישִׁית	שְׁלִישִׁי
Fourth.	רְבִיעִית	רְבִיעִי
Fifth.	חֲמִישִׁית	חֲמִישִׁי
Sixth.	שִׁשִּׁית	שִׁשִּׁי
Seventh.	שְׁבִיעִית	שְׁבִיעִי
Eighth.	שְׁמִינִית	שְׁמִינִי
Ninth.	תְּשִׁיעִית	תְּשִׁיעִי
Tenth.	עֲשִׂירִית	עֲשִׂירִי

Above ten, and sometimes even below ten, the cardinal numbers are used to express the ordinals.

בכורה 39 a	בקרת 58 a	גאון 48 b	גדרה 62 b
בכורים 50 b	בר 43 a	גאל 59 a	גוזל 35 b
בכי 43 b	ברד 47 a	גבול 34 a	גוי 34 a
בכית 45 b	ברזל 32 a	גבור 32 b	גויה 44 a
במה 59 b	בריאה 61 a	גבורה 54 b	גור 44 b
בֶּן 32 a	בריח 52 a	גבות 57 b	גורל 57 b
בֵּן 54 b	ברית 33 a	גבחת 57 b	גז 64 b
בנו 61 b	ברך 40 a	גביע 43 b	גזיר 50 a
בנות 62 b	ברכה 34 b	גביר 39 b	גזל 56 a
בני 44 b	ברק 49 b	גבלת 53 a	גזלה 56 a
בן משק 35 b	ברקת 53 a	גבעה 45 b	גזר 36 a
בעיר 44 a	בֶּשֶׂם 51 a	גבעל 47 a	גחון 31 a
בעל 35 a	בֹּשֶׂם 54 a	גבר 47 b	גחלת 57 b
בעל ברית 35 a	בשר 31 a	גברת 36 a	גי 67 b
בער 62 a	בת 32 b	גג 54 a	גיא 63 a
בערה 50 b	בת היענה 56 b	גָּד 40 a	גיד 41 a
בציר 59 a	בתולה 38 a	גַּד 49 b	גל 41 a
בצלים 60 b	בתולים 58 b	גדוד 45 a	גלגלת 49 a
בצע 42 a	בתים 52 a	גדי 39 a	גלולים 59 b
בצק 48 a	בתר 35 b	גדילים 64 b	גמא 46 a
בקע 38 b		גדיש 50 b	גמל 34 b
בקעה 34 a	**ג**	גָּדֹל 49 a	גן 30 b
בֹּקֶר 29 a	גאוה 67 b	גָּדֵל 61 a	גנב 50 a
בָּקָר 34 b	גאולה 59 a	גדר 61 b	גנבה 50 b

10*

ג

Word	Ref
גֵּךְ	50 a
גֹּפֶן	42 b
גֹּפֶר	32 b
גָּפְרִית	37 a
גֵּר	35 b
גָּרֵב	58 b
גָּרָה	46 b, 54 a
גַּרְזֶן	64 b
גֶּרֶם	45 a
גֹּרֶן .	45 b
גֵּרֵשׁ	55 a
גֵּרֵשׁ	67 a
גֶּשֶׁם	33 a

ד

Word	Ref
דָּאָה	56 b
דָּאֹבוֹן	66 a
דָּכָא	67 b
דָּכָה	41 b
דָּבָר	34 a
דֶּבֶר	46 b
דִּבְרָה	63 a
דַּבְּרָה	67 a
דְּבַשׁ	43 b
דָּג	33 b
דָּנָה	30 a
דֶּגֶל	60 a
דָּנָן	39 b
דַּד	56 a
דּוּדָאִים	40 a
דּוֹדָה	46 b
דּוּכִיפַת	56 b
דּוֹר	32 b
דּוּת	57 a
דִּיָּה	64 a
דִּין	64 b
דַּיִשׁ	59 a
דִּישֹׁן	64 a
דָּכָה	65 a
דְּלִי	62 a
דְּלֵקֶת	65 b
דֶּלֶת	37 a
דָּם	32 a
דְּמוּת	30 a
דָּמִים	50 b
דֶּמַע	50 b
דַּעַת	30 b
דַּק	49 a
דַּרְדַּר	31 b
דָּרוֹם	67 b
דְּרוֹר	59 a
דֶּרֶךְ	31 b
דֶּשֶׁא	29 b
דֶּשֶׁן	55 a
דָּת	67 a

ה

Word	Ref
הֶבֶל	66 b
הוֹד	62 a
הוֹרִים	45 b
הִין	54 a
הִלּוּלִים	58 a
הָמוֹן	36 a
הֲפֵכָה	37 a
הַר	33 a
הָרָן	31 a
הָרָר	61 b

ו

Word	Ref
וָוִים	52 a
וָלָד	34 b

ז

Word	Ref
זְאֵב	45 b
זֶבֶד	40 a
זֶבַח	41 a
זָג	60 a
זָרוֹן	64 b
זָהָב	30 b
זוֹב	57 b
זוֹלֵל	64 b
זוֹנָה	41 b
זַיִת	33 b
זָכוֹר	50 b
זָכָר	30 a
זֵכֶר	46 a
זִכָּרוֹן	48 a
זִמָּה	58 a
זְמוֹרָה	61 a
זֶמֶר	64 a
זִמְרָה	43 b
זָנָב	46 b
זְנוּנִים	42 a
זְנוּת	61 a
זֵעָה	31 b

חמור	34 b	חיק	36 a	חדש	33 a	זעוה	65 b
חמט	57 a	חכם	43 a	חוה	62 b	זעקה	36 b
חמישית	44 a	חכמה	52 b	חוט	35 b	זפת	46 a
חמנים	59 b	חלב	31 b	חול	38 a	זקונים	37 b
חמס	32 b	חלב	36 b	חומה	48 b	זקן	38 a
חמץ	48 a	חלבנה	54 b	חוף	44 b	זקן	44 a
חמץ	60 a	חלד	56 b	חוץ	32 b	זקן	57 a
חמר	34 a	חלה	53 b	חותם	42 a	זקנה	38 b.
חמר	34 b	חלום	37 b	חזה	54 a	זר	51 b
חמר	66 b	חלון	33 a	חזיר	56 a	זר	54 a
חמש	44 a	חלושה	54 b	חזק	48 a	זרא	60 b
חמת	37 b	חלי	63 b	חח	55 a	זרוע	57 a
חן	32 b, 46 a	חליפה	44 a	חטא	43 a	זרע	29 b
חנטים	45 b	חלל	41 b	חטאה	37 b	זרע	45 a
חניך	35 a	חללה	58 b	חטאים	35 a	זרת	53 a
חנכה	60 a	חלמיש	63 b	חטאת	32 a		
חסד	37 a	חלף	61 a	חטה	47 a	**ח**	
חסידה	56 b	חלצים	41 b	חטים	40 a	חבל	63 a
חסר	65 b	חלק	35 b	חי	31 b	חברה	32 a
חפזון	47 b	חלקה	39 b	חירה	60 b	חברת	52 a
חפנים	47 a	חם	33 b	חיה	30 a	חג	47 b
חפשה	58 a	חם	42 a	חיים	30 b	חגב	56 b
חץ	45 a	חמאה	36 b	חיל	41 b	חגורה	31 a
חצוצרה	60 b	חמה	39 b	חיל	48 b	חדר	43 b

66 b	כעס	54 a	כיור	53 a	ישפה	56 b	ינשוף
33 b	כף	65 a	כיס	63 b	ישר	53 b	יסוד
33 a	כֹּפֶר	57 a	כירים	52 b	יתד	52 a	יעים
49 a	כֹּפֹר	35 a	ככר	50 b	יתום	64 b	יער
51 b	כפרת	30 a	כל	44 a	יתר	61 a	יצהר
54 a	כפרים	58 a	כלאים	53 b	יתרת	44 b	יצוע
51 b	כפתר	47 b	כלב			32 b	יצר
40 b	כר	34 b	כַּלָה	**ב**		61 a	יקב
31 b	כרוב	36 b	כְּלָה	53 b	כבד	44 b	יקהה
65 a	כריתת	38 b	כלי	48 b	כברת	33 a	יקום
55 b	כרכב	66 a	כליון	40 b	כבוד	37 b	יראה
34 a	כרם	53 b	כליות	41 b	כברה	41 b	יָרֵחַ
52 b	כרמל	53 a	כליל	47 b	כביש	46 a	יֶרַח
47 b	כרעים	42 b	כן	37 b	כבשה	52 a	יריעה
40 a	כשב	32 a	כנור	37 a	כבשן	38 a	ירך
56 a	כשבה	47 a	כנם	38 a	כד	45 a	ירכה
58 a	כתבת	30 a	כנף	35 a	כהן	30 a	יָרָק
31 b	כתנת	49 b	כם	53 b	כהנה	63 b	יָרָק
52 b	כתף	43 a	כסא	50 a	כויה	65 b	ירקון
52 b	כתפת	60 a	כסוי	29 b	כוכב	62 a	יְרֵשָׁה
ל		37 b	כסות	55 a	כומז	63 a	יְרֻשָׁה
39 a	לאם	55 b	כסלים	42 b	כום	37 a	ישב
32 b	לב	47 a	כסמת	63 a	כור	45 a	ישועה
		34 b	כסף	32 a	כח	61 b	ישימון

מחמצת 48 a	מכאב 46 a	מלילת 65 a	מס 45 b
מחנה 41 a	מכבר 52 b	מליץ 43 a	מסגרת 51 b
מחנים 60 b	מכה 59 b	מלך 35 a	מסה 63 a
מחסר 64 a	מכוה 57 a	מלכות 62 a	מסה 64 a
מחצה 62 b	מכון 49 a	מלקוח 62 b	מסוה 54 b
מחצית 54 a	מכנסים 53 b	מלקוש 63 b	מסך 52 a
מחקק 44 b	מכם 62 b	מלקחים 51 b	מסכה 54 b
מחר 37 a	מכסה 33 b	ממזר 65 a	מסכנות 46 a
מחרת 37 a	מכסה 47 b	ממכר 59 a	מסכנת 63 b
מחשבה 32 b	מכר 61 a	ממכרת 59 a	מסלה 61 a
מחתה 51 b	מכרה 44 b	ממלכה 34 a	מסע 34 b
מחתרת 50 a	מכשול 58 a	ממשלה 29 b	מספד 45 b
מטה 42 a	מכשף 46 b	מן 49 b	מספוא 38 b
מטה 44 a	מכשפה 50 b	מנה 54 a	מספחת 57 a
מטוה 55 a	מכתב 54 b	מנוח 33 a	מספר 41 b
מטמון 43 b	מלא 44 a	מנוחה 45 a	מעבר 41 a
מטעמים 39 a	מלאה 50 b	מנורה 51 b	מעדנים 45 a
מטר 47 a	מלאים 53 b	מנוסה 59 b	מעון 65 a
מיטב 44 a	מלאך 36 a	מנחה 31 b	מעונן 64 b
מילדת 41 b	מלאכה 30 a	מנחש 64 b	מעט 36 b
מים 29 a	מלואה 51 a	מנים 40 b	מעיל 52 b
מין 29 b	מלון 43 b	מנעל 67 a	מעים 35 b
מישר 63 a	מלח 35 a	מנקיות 51 b	מעין 33 a
מיתרים 55 a	מלחמה 35 a	מנקת 38 b	מעל 56 a

נ

ס

	נזלים 48 b	נפלאות 46 a	סבא 64 b
	נזם 38 b	נפלים 32 b	סביבת 61 b
נאף 58 b	נזר 53 b	נפש 30 a	סבך 38 a
נאפת 58 b	נחל 39 a	נפתולים 40 a	סבלות 46 a
נאקה 46 a	נחלה 40 b	ניץ 42 b	סגלה 49 b
נביא 37 b	נָחָשׁ 31 a	נצה 55 a	סהר 42 b
נביאה 49 a	נַחַשׁ 62 a	נציב 37 a	סור 44 b
נְבֵלָה 41 a	נחשה 59 b	נקבה 30 a	סום 44 a
נְבָלָה 55 b	נחשת 32 a	נקיון 37 b	סוף 46 a
נגב 34 b	נטף 54 a	נקם 59 b	סות 44 b
נגע 34 b	נין 37 b	נקמה 62 b	סחר 38 a
נגף 48 a	נכאת 42 a	נקרה 54 b	סיר 49 a
נגש 46 a	נכד 37 b	נר 51 b	סכה 41 a
נד 48 b	נכלים 62 a	נשה 50 b	סל 42 b
נדבה 55 a	נכר 36 a	נשיא 39 b	סלם 39 b
נדה 57 a	נכרי 40 b	נשים 61 a	סלע 61 a
נדח 66 a	נס 61 b	נשך 56 b	סלעם 56 b
נדיב 61 b	נסך 41 b	נשמה 30 b	סלת 36 b
נדר 40 a	נסתרות 66 a	נשר 49 b	סמים 51 a
נהר 30 b	נעורים 33 b	נתח 53 b	סמל 63 a
נוה 48 b	נעל 35 b	נתק 57 a	סנה 46 a
נוראות 63 b	נער 36 b		סנורים 37 a
נזיד 39 a	נערה 38 a		סנפיר 56 b
נזיר 45 b	נפך 53 a	סאה 36 b	סף 48 a

11

59 b	קרי	43 a	רביד	43 b	רחמים	44 b	רצון
63 a	קריה	54 a	רביעת	35 a	ריב	62 b	רצח
38 a	קרן	54 a	רֶבַע	33 b	ריח	54 a	רֹקַח
52 a	קרסים	61 b	רֹבַע	59 b	ריק	54 a	רֹקֵחַ
60 a	קרקע	50 a	רבעים	66 a	רך	29 a	רקיע
52 a	קרש	33 b	רגל	45 a	רֹכֶב	53 b	רקיק
46 b	קיש	48 a	רגלי	45 b	רֶכֶב	52 a	רקם
60 b	קשאים	50 b	רגלים	34 b	רכוש	61 a	רֹקַע
51 b	קְשֻׁוֹת	54 b	רגע	58 a	רכיל	36 b	רֶשַׁע
60 a	קָשׂוֹת	59 b	רדף	49 b	רמה	63 b	רֵשַׁע
63 b	קשי	40 b	רהט	53 a	רמון	63 b	רִשְׁעָה
41 a	קשיטה	66 a	רוה	62 a	רֹמַח	66 b	רֶשֶׁף
56 b	קשקשת	29 a	רוּחַ	30 a	רמש	52 b	רֶשֶׁת
33 b	קֶשֶׁת	41 a	רֶוַח	30 b	רַע		שׁ
37 b	קַשָׁת	47 a	רוחה	34 a	רֵעַ		
	ר	66 b	רוש	43 a	רֹעַ	42 a	שאול
64 a	ראה	33 a	רחב	34 b	רעב	48 a	שאור
62 a	ראם	37 a	רחוב	43 a	רעבון	50 a	שאר
30 b	ראש	47 b	רחים	48 b	רעד	57 b	שארה
29 a	ראשית	40 b	רחל	44 a	רֹעָה	44 a	שארית
36 a	רב	37 b	רֶחֶם	31 b	רָעָה	31 b	שאת
41 a	רב	45 a	רַחַם	53 a	רֹעָה	53 a	שבו
66 a	רביבים	56 b	רָחָם	40 a	רעות	40 a	שבוע
		64 a	רחמה	45 b	רפא	38 a	שבועה

11*

NOUNS. 127

תחלה	43 a	תאר	40 a	שקת	38 b	שַׁעַר	37 a
תחלואים	66 a	תבה	32 b	שר	34 b	שֵׁעָר	39 a
תחמס	56 b	תבואה	44 a	שרגים	42 b	שׂערה	47 a
תחרא	53 a	תבונה	54 b	שרד	54 b	שׂערים	59 b
תחש	51 a	תבל	58 a	שרוך	35 b	שפה	34 a
תחתית	49 b	תבלל	58 b	שרט	58 a	שפחה	34 b
תימן	52 a	תבן	38 b	שרטת	58 b	שפט	36 b
תירש	39 b	תבנית	51 b	שריד	61 b	שפטים	46 b
תיש	40 a	תהו	66 a	שרף	61 a	שפי	61 b
תכלת	51 a	תהום	29 a	שרפה	34 a	שפיפון	45 a
תכן	46 b	תהלה	48 b	שרץ	29 b	שפך	55 b
תל	64 a	תהפכת	66 b	שרקה	44 b	שפכה	65 a
תלאה	49 b	תודה	56 a	שררות	66 a	שפלה	63 a
תלי	39 a	תוך	29 a	שרש	66 a	שפם	57 b
תלנת	49 a	תולדות	30 a	שרשרת	52 b	שפן	56 a
תם	37 b	תולעים	49 a	שרשת	53 a	שפע	67 b
תמהון	65 b	תולעת	51 a	שש	43 a	שֶׁפֶר	45 a
תמול	40 b	תומים	39 a	שתי	57 b	שֹׁפָר	49 b
תמונה	50 a	תועבה	43 b			שק	42 a
תמורה	59 b	תועפת	62 a	ת		שקדים	43 b
תמים	53 a	תוצאת	62 b	תאו	64 a	שקוץ	63 a
תמר	49 a	תור	35 b	תאוה	31 a	שקל	38 a
תנואה	61 a	תורה	39 a	תאמים	42 a	שקץ	56 a
תנובה	66 b	תושב	38 a	תאנה	31 a	שקר	46 b

INDEX TO THE VERBS.

	ב		אנף	91 a		אזל	93 b
			אסף	71 b		[5] אזן	71 a
83 a	אבד	91 a	[3] באר	79 b	אסר	75 a	אחז
90 b	[3] אבר	79 a	באש	85 b	אפד	78 b	[2] אחז
75 b	אבה	84 b	בגד	74 b	אפה	76 a	אחר
79 b	[7] אבל	68 a	[5] בדל	81 a	אפס	85 a	איב
78 b	[2] אבק	80 b	[2] בדל	80 b	[7] אפק	69 b	אכל
92 b	אגר	71 b	בוא	76 b	אצל	79 a	[3] אלם
85 a	אדם	69 b	[5] בוא	92 a	ארב	73 b	[5] אמן
83 b	[2] אדר	83 b	[2] בוך	76 a	ארד	76 a	אמץ
75 a	אהב	70 a	בוש	70 a	ארר	68 a	אמר
73 a	אהל	86 a	[3] בוש	85 a	[3] ארש	92 b	[5] אמר
89 a	[7] אוה	76 a	בזה	87 a	אשם	84 b	[3] אנה
74 b	אוץ	79 a	בז	77 a	[3] אשר	82 a	[2] אנח
69 a	אור	80 a	בחן	93 b	אתה	89 a	[7] אנן

71 a	בחר	69 a	[3] ברך	75 a	גמל	84 a	דמם
87 a [3]	בטא	79 b	בשל	77 b	גנב	78 b	דפק
92 b	בטח	73 b	בתר	88 b	געל	90 b	דקר
93 a	בין		**ג**	79 a	גער	90 b	דרך
75 a	בכה			91 a [7]	גרה	72 a	דרש
92 a [3]	בכר	83 b	גאה	90 b [3]	גרם	68 b [5]	דשא
89 b [4]	בכר	81 a	גאל	82 b	גרע	93 a	דשן
74 a	בלה	84 b	גבל	87 b	גרר	85 b [3]	דשן
72 b	בלל	71 b	גבר	70 b	גרש		**ה**
80 a	בלע	91 b [7]	גדד		**ד**	90 b	הדף
70 a	בנה	72 b	גדל			85 a	הדר
93 a	בעט	91 b [3]	גדע	85 a	דאב	76 b	הוה
74 b	בעל	89 b [3]	גדף	76 b	דאה	91 a [5]	הון
82 a	בער	81 b	גוד	91 a	דבק	68 a	היה
84 b [3]	בער	89 b	גוז	77 b	[5] דבק	69 b	הלך
84 b [5]	בער	71 b	גוע	72 a	[3] דבר	72 b [3]	הלל
91 b	בצק	72 b	גור	81 b	דגה	83 b	המם
72 b	בצר	77 b	גזז	89 b	דוך	89 b [5]	הסה
71 b	בקע	75 a	גזל	71 a	דון	70 b	הפך
87 b [3]	בקר	72 a	גלה	92 b	דוש	70 b	הרג
78 a [3]	בקש	80 a	[3] גלח	71 a	דין	70 b	הרה
68 a	ברא	77 a	גלל	82 a	דלה	70 b	הרס
73 b	ברח	80 b	[7] גלל	78 a	דלק	83 b	הרס
75 b	ברך	75 b	[5] גמא	90 b [3]	דמה	77 b [3]	התל

75 b [5] חרש	78 b [3] טמא	70 b ילד	69 b יצר
86 a חרת	79 a טמן	71 a [2] ילד	87 a יקד
73 b חשב	81 a טען	82 a [3] ילד	78 b יקע
74 b חשך	72 a טרף	89 a [7] ילד	90 b [5] יקע
83 a חשך	**י**	72 a ילך	72 a יקץ
77 b חשף		82 a [5] ילך	91 b [2] יקש
78 b חשק	89 b [2] יאל	73 a [5] ימן	70 a ירא
93 b חתם	74 a [5] יאל	85 a [5] ינה	72 b ירד
88 a [5] חתם	78 b יאת	69 b [5] ינח	75 b [5] ירד
78 b [7] חתן	79 b [3] יבם	75 a ינק	78 a ירה
91 a [2] חתת	72 a יבש	83 a יסד	81 a [5] ירה
ט	91 b יגר	86 a יסך	90 a ירט
	77 a [5] ידה	70 b יסף	75 a ירע
80 b טבח	87 a [7] ידה	89 a [3] יסר	89 b ירק
79 b טבל	70 a ידע	84 b יער	73 a ירש
83 b טבע	77 a יהב	85 b [2] יער	80 b [2] ירש
87 b טהר	81 b יחד	84 a יעץ	92 b [3] ירש
87 b [3] טהר	72 a יחל	93 b [5] יפע	71 a ישב
79 a [7] טהר	77 b יחם	90 b יצא	81 b ישם
89 a [5] טוב	72 b יטב	68 b [5] יצא	70 a ישן
86 b טוה	70 b [5] יטב	82 a [7] יצב	87 b [2] ישן
88 a טוח	74 b [2] יכח	77 b [5] יצג	89 a [2] ישע
86 a טחן	75 a [5] יכח	83 a [6] יצג	82 a [5] ישע
87 b טמא	73 a יכל	77 a יצק	90 a ישר

נטיש 78 a	נדח [5] 91 b	משל 69 a	מלח [4] 86 a
נכה [5] 71 a	נדף [2] 89 a	מישש [3] 78 a	מלט [2] 74 b
נכל [3] 90 b	נדר 77 a	מתק 84 a	מלך 79 a
נכל [7] 79 a	נהג 77 b		מלל [3] 75 a
נכר [3] 93 b	נהל 78 b	**נ**	מלק 87 a
נכר [5] 76 b	נוא [5] 90 b	נאם 75 b	כנה 73 a
נכר [7] 80 a	נוד 70 b	נאף 84 b	מנע 77 a
נמל 73.b	נוה [5] 83 b	נאץ 80 b	מסם [2] 84 a
נסג [5] 92 a	נוח 71 b	נבא [7] 89 b	מסר 90 b
נסה [3] 75 a	נוס 73 a	נבב 85 b	מעט 83 a
נסח [2] 93 a	נוע 70 b	נבט [5] 73 a	מעל 87 a
נסך 79 a	נוף [5] 84 b	נבל 84 a	מצא 69 b
נסע 72 b	נזה 86 a	נבל [3] 93 a	מצא [5] 87 b
נעם 81 b	נזל 90 b	נגד [5] 70 a	מצה 87 a
נער [3] 83 b	נזר [2] 88 b	נגח 84 b	מקק [2] 89 a
נפח 69 b	נזר [5] 88 a	נגע 70 a	מרד 73 a
נפל 70 a	נחה 76 a	נגע [5] 77 a	מרה 90 a
נפל [7] 80 b	נחל 85 a	נגף 82 b	מרט [2] 87 b
נפץ 72 a	נחם [2] 71 a	נגש 82 b	מרק [4] 87 b
נפש [2] 85 a	נחם [3] 71 a.	נגש 74 a	מרר 81 b
נצב [2] 73 b	נחש [3] 77 b	נגש [5] 76 b	מרר [5] 85 a
נצב [5] 75 a	נטה 72 b	נדב 85 a	משה 82 a
נצה [2] 82 a	נטע 69 b	נדד 78 a	משח 77 b
נצל [2] 78 b	נטר 88 a	נדח 91 a	משך 79 a

71 a	עצב		**פ**	80 a	[2] פעם	71 b	פתח
76 b	עצם			70 b	פצה	76 a	[3] פתח
73 b	עצר	93 b	[5] פאה	77 b	[3] פצל	77 a	[2] פתל
76 b	עקב	92 b	[3] פאר	92 a	פצע	79 b	פתר
75 a	עקד	82 b	[7] פאר	74 a	פצר	87 a	פתת
81 b	[3] עקר	75 b	פגע	75 a	פקר		
80 b	ערב	78 b	פגש	79 b	[5] פקד		**צ**
75 b	[3] ערה	83 b	פדה	70 a	פקח	86 b	צבא
88 b	[5] ערה	81 a	פוג	69 b	[2] פרד	89 a	צבה
73 a	ערך	72 a	פוץ	77 b	[5] פרד	80 a	צבר
88 b	ערל	81 b	פזז	69 a	פרה	84 b	צדה
83 b	[2] ערם	93 a	פחד	83 a	פרח	79 b	צדק
83 b	ערף	74 a	[2] פלא	87 b	פרם	85 a	[5] צדק
91 a	ערץ	88 b	[3] פלא	87 b	[5] פרם	80 b	[7] צדק
68 b	עשה	89 b	[5] פלא	82 b	פרע	76 b	צוד
84 b	עשן	72 b	[2] פלג	77 a	פרץ	69 b	[3] צוה
87 a	עשק	82 b	[5] פלה	76 b	פרק	91 b	[5] צוף
76 b	[7] עשק	81 a	[3] פלל	73 b	[5] פרר	90 a	צוץ
77 a	[3] עשר	74 b	[7] פלל	83 a	פרש	93 a	[5] צוק
73 a	[5] עשר	74 a	פנה	88 b	פרש	85 a	צור
72 b	[5] עתק	76 a	[3] פנה	87 b	פשה	73 b	צחק
76 a	עבר	83 a	פסח	87 a	פשט	75 b	צלח
		86 b	פסל	79 a	[5] פשט	84 a	צלל
		84 a	פעל	72 a	פתה	78 b	צלע

			ש			
שׂכֵל [5]	70 a	שׁוט	89 a	שׁאב	75 b	רכס	85 b
שכם [5]	74 a	שׁום	69 b	שׁאה [7]	75 b	רכשׁ	72 b
שׁכן	70 b	שׁוף	70 a	שׁאל	76 a	רמה	83 b
שׂכר	72 a	שׁור	90 a	שׁאל [5]	83 b	רמה [3]	77 a
שׂכר	77 a	שׁושׁ	93 a	שׁאר [2]	71 b	רמם [2]	90 a
שׁלב [4]	85 b	שׁות	70 a	שׁאר [5]	83 a	רמם [3]	83 b
שׁלח	70 b	שׁזר [6]	85 b	שׁכה	73 a	רמשׁ	69 a
שׁלך [5]	75 a	שׁחה [7]	73 b	שׁבע	84 a	רנן	87 b
שׁלם [3]	80 b	שׁחט	75 a	שׂבע [2]	75 a	רעב	80 a
שׁלם [5]	92 a	שׂחט	79 b	שׂבע [5]	75 b	רעה	77 a
שׁלף	90 a	שׂחק	86 a	שׁבץ [3]	85 b	רעץ	83 b
שׁלשׁ [3]	92 a	שׁחת [3]	71 b	שׁבר	74 b	רפא	74 b
שׂמאל [5]	73 a	שׁטה	89 a	שׁבת	69 a	רפה	82 b
שׁמד [2]	79 a	שׁטח	89 b	שׁגב	91 a	רצה	78 b
שׁמד [5]	89 a	שׁטם	76 b	שׁגג	87 a	רצח	84 b
שׁמח	82 b	שׁטף	87 b	שׁגה	87 a	רצע	84 b
שׁמט	85 a	שׁיר	83 b	שׁגל	92 b	רצץ	92 b
שׁמם	81 a	שׁכב	74 b	שׂדף	79 b	רצץ [7]	76 a
שׁמן	93 a	שׁכח	77 a	שׁוב	70 b	רקח	86 a
שׁמע	70 a	שׁכך	71 b	שׁוב [5]	74 b	רקע	86 b
שׁמר	69 b	שׂכך	86 b	שׁור	92 b	רקק	88 a
שׁמר [2]	75 b	שׂכל	77 a	שׁוח	76 a	רשׁע [5]	84 b
שׂנא	76 b	שׂכל [3]	78 a				
שׁנה	80 a	שׂכל [3]	81 a				

12*

INDEX TO THE⁖PARTICLES.

- אמת 104 a
- אנה 97 a
- אנא 99 b
- אף 95 a
- אפוא 98 a
- אפיל 100 a
- אפס 103 b
- אצל 99 a
- ארגמן 103 a
- ארך 101 b
- אשר 94 a
- את 94 a, 95 b

ב

- בבלי 104 a
- בגלל 96 b
- בדד 102 b
- בהו 94 a
- בזה 99 a
- בחור 100 a
- בטח 98 b
- בי 99 b
- בין 94 a
- בכור 97 a
- בליעל 104 a
- בלעדי 96 b
- בלתי 97 b
- בעבור 95 b
- בעד 96 a
- בצור 103 b
- ברוד 98 b
- בריא 99 a
- בשגם 95 b
- בשל 100 a
- בֶּשֶׁם 101 b
- כְּשֶׁם 101 b

ג

- גבה 96 a
- גבח 102 a
- גבן 102 b
- גדול 94 b
- גזול 105 a
- גזרה 102 b
- גלוי 104 b
- גם 95 a

ד

- דוה 102 b
- די 101 b
- דל 99 a
- דק 99 a
- דרור 101 b

ה

- הא 99 b
- האל 97 a
- הבה 96 a
- הדק 101 b
- הדר 103 b
- הוא 95 a
- היא 95 a
- היטב 104 a
- הכי 98 a
- הלאה 97 a
- הלזה 97 b
- הלם 97 a
- הן 95 b
- הִנֵּה 94 b
- הֵנָּה 97 b
- הרבה 96 b
- הרה 97 a
- הרחק 97 b

ז.

- זאת 95 a
- זב 102 b
- זה 95 a
- זולתי 104 a
- זך 101 a
- זקן 97 a
- זר 101 a

ח

- חרש 99 a
- חום 98 b
- חוש 104 b
- חזק 100 a
- חי 94 b
- חיים 100 b
- חכלילי 99 b
- חכם 99 a
- חל 102 a
- חלוץ 104 b

100 b	מוּל	105 a	מְשֻׁגָּע	99 a	נָכוֹן	עַל-אוֹדֹת	97 b
104 a	מוּל	102 a	מָשִׁיחַ	99 a	נָכְרִי	עַל-בְּלִי	98 b
98 b	מִזֶּה	96 b	מְשֻׁלָּשׁ	105 a	נִפְלָא	עָלַי	104 b
105 b	מָזֶה	99 a	מִשְׁנֶה	98 a	נָקוֹד	עֶלְיוֹן	96 b
100 b	מַחְסְפָּס	101 a	מִשְׁקָד	100 a	נִרְפָּה	עַל-כֵּן	95 a
95 a	מִי	96 b	מַשְׁקֶה	103 a	נִתּוּק	עַל-פִּי	99 a
97 b	מָלֵא	98 a	מָתַי			עִם	95 a
102 b	מְמֵאִיר		**ס**			עִמָּדִי	95 b
101 b	מִמֶּלַח		**נ**			עֵמֶק	102 a
97 b	מִמַּעַל	96 a	נָא	97 b	סָבִיב	עֹנֶג	105 a
95 a	מִן	100 b	נָאְדָּר	104 b	סוֹרֵר	עָנוּ	103 a
100 b	מָן	103 b	נֶאֱמָן			עָנִי	100 b
103 a	מָעוֹךְ	101 a	נָבוּב		**ע**		
99 b	מְעַט	100 a	נָבוֹךְ	103 b	עֵבֹת	עָצוּם	97 a
103 a	מַעֲלָה	99 a	נָבוֹן	95 b	עַד	עֶצֶם	96 a
96 a	מִפְּנֵי	105 b	נָבָל	100 b	עַד-אָנָה	עָקֵב	97 b
97 a	מִצְעָר	100 b	נָנַח	96 b	עַד-הֵנָּה	עָקוֹד	98 b
99 b	מְצֹרָע	104 b	נָנַף	104 b	עֲדִי	עָקָר	96 a
101 a	מַקְשֶׁה	102 b	נִדָּה	95 b	עוֹד	עִקֵּשׁ	105 a
98 a	מַר	104 b	נִדָּח	100 a	עוֹר	עָרוֹם	95 a
104 b	מָרָה	101 b	נָדִיב	99 b	עַז	עֲרִירִי	96 b
102 b	מָרוּחַ	98 a	נוֹרָא	98 b	עָטוּף	עָרֵל	100 a
105 b	מְרִירִי	95 a	נֶחְמָד	98 a	עִיף	עָרֵם	95 a
105 b	מָרַר	96 a	נִיחֹחַ	95 a	עֵירֹם	עָשׁוֹק	104 b
				94 a	עַל	עָשִׁיר	101 b

APPENDIX.

A literal version of three chapters from the Pentateuch: the first of Genesis, and the fifteenth and twentieth of Exodus, intended to exhibit, as far as practicable, and as far as these three chapters go, the true idiom of the Hebrew language. The words are, for this purpose, not transposed, but the rendering of each is given separately without regard to the connection in which it stands with others, and placed between perpendicular lines. To this end, also, we have, in some instances, deviated even from our own renderings given in the Vocabulary.

The word את, whether it has a prefix or pronominal affix joined to it or not, is represented by a horizontal line. In regard to that word, see note on page 94.

Where the constructed state of the noun is indicated in the Hebrew by a change of vowel points, or otherwise, the word *of* appears in the same type as the rest; but where it is not expressed in the original text, but merely understood, it is given in Italics.

(143)

GENESIS I.

(1.) In beginning | he created | Gods* | — | the heavens† | and — | the earth | (2) And the earth | she was | waste | and void | and darkness | upon | face of | abyss | and spirit *of* | Gods | hovering | upon | face of | the waters | (3) And he said | Gods | he shall be | light | and he was | light | (4) And he saw | Gods | — | the light | that | good | and he caused to divide | Gods | between | the light | and between | the darkness | (5) And. he called | Gods | to the light | day | and to the darkness | he called | night | and he was | evening | and he was | morning | day |* one | (6) And he said | Gods .| he shall be | expansion | in midst of | the waters | and he shall be | causing to divide | between | waters | to the waters | (7) And he made | Gods | — | the expansion | and he caused to divide | between | the waters | which | from beneath | to the expansion | and

* We have rendered this word, as also, *heavens, waters,* and other similar words in the plural, because they assume this form in Hebrew. It is not to be inferred, however, that this implies a plurality of objects. The Hebrew idiom admits of a peculiar use of the plural form denoting extent, greatness, dignity, or majesty, technically called *pluralis excellentiæ;* or representing abstract ideas, in distinction of objects, the limits of which may be wholly comprehended by the senses. Thus, for instance, חשכים *darkness* (Isa. 50: 10); עולמים *eternity* (Isa. 26: 4; 45: 17); אהבים and דרים *love* (Prov. 7: 18); תהמת and מצולת *abyss, unfathomable depth* (Ex. 15: 5), are often used in the plural. To titles of the Most High, it is therefore particularly and very generally applied, and frequently, also, to earthly rulers, as האיש אדני הארץ *the man, the lords of the land* (Gen. 42: 30), and several other instances.

† The Hebrew words for *heavens* and *waters* have the dual form.

between | the waters | which | from above | to the expansion | and he was | so | (8) And he called | Gods | to the expansion | heavens | and he was | evening | and he was| morning | day | second | (9) And he said | Gods | they shall be gathered | the waters | from beneath | the heavens | to | place | one | and she shall be seen | the dry | and he was | so | (10) And he called | Gods | to the dry | land | and to gathering of | the waters | he called | seas | and he saw | Gods | that | good | (11) And he said | Gods| she shall cause to grass | the earth | grass | herb | causing to seed | seed | tree of | fruit | making | fruit | for his kind | which | his seed | in him | upon | the earth | and he was | so | (12) And she caused to come out | the earth| grass | herb | causing to seed | seed | for his kind | and tree | making | fruit | which | his seed | in him | for his kind | and he saw | Gods | that | good | (13) And he was| evening | and he was | morning | day | third | (14) And he said | Gods | he shall be | lighters | in expansion of | the heavens | to cause to divide | between | the day | and between | the night | and they shall be | for signs | and for appointed times | and for days | and years | (15) And they shall be | for lighters | in expansion of | the heavens| to cause to light | upon | the earth | and he was | so | (16) And he made | Gods | — | two of | the lighters | the large | — | the lighter | the large | to ruling of | the day| and — | the lighter | the small | to ruling of | the night | and — | the stars | (17) And he placed | — them | Gods | in expansion of | the heavens | to cause to light | upon | the earth | (18) And to rule | in the day | and in the night | and to cause to divide | between | the light | and

13

between | the darkness | and he saw | Gods | that | good|
(19) And he was | evening | and he was | morning | day|
fourth | (20) And he said | Gods | they shall reptile* |
the water | reptile | animal | living | and fowl | he shall
fly | upon | the earth | upon | face of | expansion of | the
heavens | (21) And he created | Gods | — | the sea-mon-
sters | the large | and — | all | animal | the . living | the
creeping | which | they reptiled | the waters | to their
kind |.and — | all | fowl *of* | wing | to his kind | and he
saw | Gods | that | good | (22) And he blessed | — them|
Gods | to say | be ye fruitful | and increase ye | and fill
ye | — | the waters | in the seas | and the fowl | he shall
increase | in the earth | (23) And he was | evening | and
he was | morning | day | fifth | (24) And he said | Gods |
she shall cause to come out | the earth | animal | living |
to her kind | cattle | and creeping things | and living crea-
tures of | earth | to her kind | and he was | so | (25) And
he made | Gods | — | living creatures of | the earth ·| to
her kind | and — | the cattle | to her kind | and — | all |
creeping things of | the ground | to his kind | and he saw|
Gods | that | good | (26) And he said | Gods | we shall
make | human being | in our image | like our likeness |
and they shall rule | over fishes of | the sea | and over
fowl *of* | the heavens | and over the cattle | and over all |
the earth | and over all | the creeping things | the creep-
ing | upon | the earth | (27) And he created | Gods | — |
the human being | in his image | in image *of* | Gods | he

---

* In close imitation of the Hebrew, we have sometimes taken the
liberty of using such a verb, though illegitimate, in order to represent
more truly the idiom of the original.

created | — him | male | and female | he created | — them |
(28) And he blessed | — them | Gods | and he said | to
them | Gods | be ye fruitful | and increase ye | and fill
ye | — | the earth | and subject her | and rule ye | over
fishes of | the sea | and over fowl *of* | the heavens | and
over all | living creature | the creeping | upon | the earth |
(29) And he said | Gods | behold | I have given | to you |
— | all | herb | seeding | seed | which | upon | face of |
all | the earth | and — | all | the tree | which | in him |
fruit *of* | tree | seeding | seed | to you | he shall be | for
food | (30) And to all | living creatures of | the earth |
and to all | fowl *of* | the heavens | and to all | creeping |
upon | the earth | which | in him | soul | living | — | all |
greenness *of* | herb | for food | and he was | so | (31) And
he saw | Gods | — | all | which | he made | and behold |
good | very | and he was | evening | and he was | morn-
ing | day | the sixth |

EXODUS XV.

(1) Then | he shall sing* | Moses | and sons of | Israel |
— | the song | the this | to Yehovah | and they said |
to say | I shall sing | to Yehovah | for | to exalt | he ex-
alted | horse | and his rider | he cast | in the sea | (2) My
strength | and song | Yah | and he was | to me | to salva-
tion | this | my God | and I will glorify him | Gods of |
my father | and I will exalt him | (3) Yehovah | man *of* |
war | Yehovah | his name | (4) Chariots of | Pharao |

* The future is here used for the past

and his army | he cast | in the sea | and choicest of | his
wariors | they are sunk | in sea of | weed | (5) Abysses |
they shall cover* them | they went down | in depths |
like | stone | (6) Thy right | Yehovah | glorious | in
strength | thy right | Yehovah | she shall crush* | enemy |
(7) And in abundance of | thy exaltedness | thou shalt
overthrow* | thy risers up | thou shalt send* | thy burn-
ing | he shall consume them | like stubble | (8) And with
breath *of* | thy nostrils | they were heaped up | waters |
they were set up | like | heap | floods | they congealed |
abysses | in heart of | sea | (9) He said | enemy | I shall | pursue
I shall overtake | I shall divide | spoil | she shall fill them | my
soul † | I shall draw | my sword | she shall cause them to pos-
sess | my hand | (10) Thou didst blow | with thy wind | he
covered them | sea | they rolled down | like lead | in waters |
mighty | (11) Who | like thee | among mighty ones |
Yehovah | who | like thee | glorious | in holiness | fearful |
praises | doing | wonder | (12) Thou didst extend | thy
right | she shall swallow* them | earth | (13) Thou didst
lead | with thy favor | people | this | thou didst deliver |
thou didst lead | with thy strength | to | habitation of |
thy holiness | (14) They heard | peoples | they shall trem-
ble* | fear | he seized | dwellers of | Palestine | (15) Then |
they were terrified | chiefs of | Edom | mighty ones of |
Moab | he shall seize them | trembling | they melted |
all | dwellers of | Canaan | (16) She shall fall | upon them |
fear | and dread | with greatness of | thy arm | they
shall be still | like stone | until | he shall pass | thy

---

* The future is here used for the past.
† *i. e.* My courage, my vengeance.

people | Yehovah | until | he shall pass | people | this |
thou hast possessed |(17) Thou shalt bring them | and thou
shalt plant them | on mountain *of* | thy possession | place|
for thy dwelling | thou hast made | Yehovah | sanctuary|
my Lords | they established | thy hands | (18) Yehovah |
he shall reign | to eternity | and ever | (19) For | he
came | horse *of* | Pharao | with his chariot | and with his
horsemen | in the sea | and he caused to return | Yehovah|
on them | — | waters of | the sea | and sons of | Israel |
they went | on the dry | in midst of | the sea | (20) And
she took|Miriam | the prophetess | sister of | Aaron | —|
the timbrel | in her hand | and they went out | all | the
women | after her | with timbrels | and with dances |
(21) And she spoke ↲ to them | Miriam | sing ye | to
Yehovah | for | to exalt | he exalted | horse | and his
rider | he cast |`in the sea | (22) And he caused to journey|
Moses | — | Israel | from sea of | weed | and they went
out | to | wilderness of | Shur | and they went | three of|
days | in the wilderness | and not | they found | waters |
(23) And they came | to Marah | and not | they could | to
drink | waters | from Marah | for | bitter | they | upon |
so | he called | her name | Marah | (24) And they mur-
mured | the people | upon | Moses | to . say | what | we
shall drink | (25) And he cried | to | Yehovah | and he
caused to direct him | Yehovah | tree | and he caused to
cast | to | the waters | and they were sweet | the waters|
there | he placed | for him | statute | and judgment |
and there | he tried him | (26) And he said |.if.|·to hear |
thou shalt hear | to voice *of* | Yehovah | thy Gods | and
the just | in his eyes | thou shalt do | and thou shalt cause

to hear | to his commandments | and thou shalt keep |
all | his statutes | all | the disease | which | I placed | in
Egypt | not | I will place | upon thee | for | I | Yehovah |
thy healer | (27) And they came | to Elim | and there |
two of | ten | wells of | waters | and seventy | dates | and
they encamped | there | by | the waters |

EXODUS XX.

(1) And he spoke | Gods | — | all | the words | the
these | to say | (2) I | Yehovah | thy Gods | which | I
have caused thee to go out | from land of | Egypt | from
house of | slaves | (3) Not | he shall be | to thee | Gods |
others | by | my faces | (4) Not | thou shalt make | for
thee | graven thing | and all | likeness | which | in the
heavens | from above | and which | in the earth | from
beneath | and which | in the waters | from beneath | to
the earth | (5) Not | thou shalt prostrate thyself | to them |
and not | thou shalt serve them | for | I | Yehovah | thy
Gods | God | jealous | visiting | sin of | fathers | upon |
sons | upon | third ones | and upon | fourth ones | to my
haters | (6) And doing | favor | to thousands | to my
lovers | and to keepers of | my commandments | (7) Not |
thou shalt bear | — | name *of* | Yehovah | thy Gods | for
falsehood | for | not | he shall let free | — | which | he
shall bear | — | his name | for falsehood | (8) Remem-
ber | — | day *of* | the sabbath | to sanctify him | (9) Six
of | days | thou shalt labor | and thou shalt do | all | thy

work | (10) And day | the seventh | sabbath | to Yeho-
vah | thy Gods | not | thou shalt do | all | labor | thou |
and thy son | and thy daughter | thy slave | and thy fe-
male slave | and thy cattle | and thy stranger | which |
in thy gates | (11) For | six of | days | he made | Yeho-
vah | — | the heavens | and—. | the earth | — | the sea |
and — | all | which | in them | and he rested | on the day|
the seventh | upon | so | he blessed | Yehovah | — | day|
the sabbath | and he sanctified him | (12) Honor | — | thy
father | and — | thy mother | in order that | they shall be
long | thy days | upon | the earth | which | Yehovah | thy
Gods | he gives | to thee | (13) Not | thou shalt murder |
(14) Not | thou shalt commit adultery | (15) Not | thou
shalt steal | (16) Not | thou shalt speak | against thy fel-
low | witness *of* | falsehood | (17) Not | thou shalt covet |
house of | thy fellow | not | thou shalt covet | wife of |
thy fellow | and his slave | and his female slave | and his
ox | and his ass | and all | which | to thy fellow | (18) And
all | the people | seeing | — | the voices. | and — | the
flames | and — | voice *of* | the cornet | and— | the moun-
tain | smoking | and he saw | the people | and they
moved | and they stood | from afar | (19) And they said|
to | Moses | speak | thou | with us | and we shall hear |
and not | he shall speak | with us | Gods | lest | we shall
die | (20) And he said | Moses | to | the people | not | ye
shall fear | for | in order that | to try |—you | he came|the
Gods | and in order that | she shall be | his fear | upon |
your faces | not to | ye shall sin | (21) And he stood | the
people f from afar | and Moses | he approached | to | the
thick darkness | which | there | the Gods | (22) And he

said | Yehovah | to | Moses | thus | thou shalt say | to |
sons of | Israel | ye | ye have seen | that | from | the hea-
vens | I have spoken | with you | (23) Not | ye shall
make | with me | gods of | silver | and gods of | gold |
not | ye shall make | to you | (24) Altar of | earth. | thou
shalt make | for me | and thou shalt slaughter | upon
him | — | thy offerings | and — | thy peace offerings | — |
thy small cattle | and — | thy large cattle | in all | the
place | which | I shall remember | — | my name | I shall
come | to thee | and I shall bless thee | (25) And if | altar
of | stones | ye shall make | for me | not | ye shall build |
them | hewn | for | thy sword | thou didst raise | upon
her | and thou didst pollute her | (26) And not | thou shalt
ascend | with steps | upon | my altar | which | not | she
shall be uncovered | thy nakedness | upon him |

THE END.

www.ingramcontent.com/pod-product-compliance
Lightning Source LLC
Chambersburg PA
CBHW030556270326
41927CB00007B/940